TECHNOLOGY—
THE GOD THAT FAILED

Technology—
The God That Failed

By
DOROTHY M. SLUSSER
and
GERALD H. SLUSSER

W

THE WESTMINSTER PRESS

Philadelphia

ISBN 0–664–24909–4

Library of Congress Catalog Card No. 78–138818

Book Design by
Dorothy Alden Smith

Published by The Westminster Press ®
Philadelphia, Pennsylvania

PRINTED IN THE UNITED STATES OF AMERICA

CONTENTS

TECHNOLOGY—
THE GOD THAT FAILED

INTRODUCTION

The modern technological society is an incredibly vast experiment without historical precedent. The three hundred million years of natural experimentation before the advent of man had produced a beautifully complex and delicately balanced world which was successfully re-generative—a world that could "last." Man first began seriously to tamper with the delicate balance of nature when he invented agriculture, but with the advent of modern technology, his experiments have assumed such enormous proportions that he now stands on the threshold of destroying the world's ability to support life.

Man has learned to *believe* that experimentation is good; it leads to knowledge and to technology which will improve life. While aware that experimentation always involves some risk, scientific man determines to run those risks, both known and estimated, because of the expected value of what may be learned. But as Jules Henri Poincaré has said: "The first determination to submit to experiment is not enough; there are still dangerous hypotheses; first, and above all, those which are tacit and unconscious. Since we make them without knowing it, we are powerless to abandon them." This book is about a number of those dangerous hypotheses which are at work in the various developed technological social orders of the world, but particularly those in the United States.

That the technological order is based on unproved hypotheses is known by scholars and scientists, although some often are forgotten or unnoticed, but that knowledge is usually not part of the public or political intelligence. These hyptheses are of various natures: theological, social, and scientific. The major result of them, so far as their immediate danger is concerned, is best seen in the mounting environmental crisis. Man's arrogant disregard of the finite cyclical nature of the planet he inhabits threatens to make that planet hostile to all forms of life.

A horrifying example of one of the dangerous hypotheses is the tacit belief that the oceans are so vast we can endlessly dump our wastes into them without fear of destroying their capacity to support life. As a result, man is dumping into the oceans thousands of products without giving thought to possible negative biological consequences. For example, the Atomic Energy Commission has been mixing vast amounts of radioactive wastes with concrete, loading them into ordinary steel drums and dumping them into the Atlantic. The British have simplified their disposal by merely running a pipeline two miles out from shore, assuming that it is safe to discharge one hundred thousand curies of radioactive wastes through it per month. (A curie is the amount of radioactivity produced per second by one gram of radium.) The quantity of radioactivity environmentally tolerable is limited and cannot be used twice, making our nuclear experiments suspiciously irresponsible.

Another example is found in the report that the Dow Chemical Company has dumped up to two hundred pounds of mercury per day for the last forty years into Lake St. Clair in Canada, innocent, they say, of the fact that mercury undergoes a poisonous transformation in water through the action of bacteria. Lake St. Clair is only a single example. Since 1953 at least 110 people have been poisoned, some fatally, from eating fish around Minamata Bay, Japan. The Baltic Sea is so contaminated with mercury poisoning that most of its fish are inedible and some investigators are saying that the entire Mississippi should be off limits. Four states, widely scattered, have shut down their lakes and rivers to fishing, while sixteen others have found dangerous levels of mercury in their fish and drinking water.

This book is, then, concerned with the ecological crisis resulting from modern industrial man's worship of the god Technology. It concerns the creation of that god, the nature of its failure, and the theological implications for the world. In particular, we are concerned to make the "tacit and unconscious" both explicit and conscious, so far as the making of the technological world and its environmental disaster are concerned. The development of the book proceeds by surveying the evolution of a culture dominated by science and technology, examining particular environmental damage resulting from that technology, and concluding with an examination of man's attitude toward the natural world and a suggestion of a more adequate relationship to that world than his technological positivism is able to provide.

1

THE ETIOLOGY OF CANCER

When God decided to invent the world, said e. e. cummings, he took a breath bigger than a circus tent and everything began. Suddenly, in the nowhere, for there was neither time nor even empty space, hydrogen atoms began to appear and with them space, gravity, time, and all the configurations of relativity. Perhaps eons later, when novas had been formed by the collective gravitational impulses of the hydrogen, one nova chose to explode and in the beauty of its expansive, shining death all the material elements were formed. It is these cosmic events which provide the building blocks for the stuff of our solar system, earth, and life. This is our history, our beginning and becoming. This is the wonder of all wonders and joy of all joys, that the good green earth is here and that the universe yearns to give life to its creatures!

Man is inextricably part and parcel of the universe, but many have forgotten or overlooked it in their haste to build a world encompassed only by man's technology. Thus, many well-educated "modern" men speak of man *and* nature, or man's *conquest* of nature. They are assuming some great division over which man has passed, leaving behind all other creatures and things. Theologians, both ancient and modern, have done their part to support this magnanimous illusion with its ego-building effect. Yet, as the following pages will demonstrate, it is a most fateful illusion, for it has allowed or even encouraged man to overlook or ignore the necessities of his intimate relation to and dependence upon the remainder of the environment.

Man is a very late comer to the earth and presumably to the universe, though we can speak with only modest assurance on this latter point. If the earth, metaphorically speaking, is just now entering the second day of its existence, then man arrived at one second before midnight. The table at which he was to feast was all prepared by hands other than his own, and the companions on his journey were already present before man arrived. For eons of time the earth turned in silence with no sentient life to respond to its providence. Then in some stretch of water, in a warm salt sea, cellular life appeared amid conditions that would allow it to live and multiply. How did it happen? To that question there are no final answers, although many theories, and there may never be answers for man. Some simply say, "God willed it"; others seek for a less beautiful but more provable answer. Whatever its source, life began in the biosphere of earth and began that process of reverse entropy which makes, at least for the duration of the organism, a lie of the second law of thermodynamics. Thermodynamically speaking, life has no right to be. It collects rather than scatters energy. It moves away from simplicity toward complexity and diversification. Life reaches out from within itself. There is an inexplicable drive within all living things that has pushed on to the limits of the biosphere. Where did that contagious impulse come from? What does it mean? Was the scientist Arrhenius right in thinking that the spores of life came originally from outer space? But if so, how did they get there? The secret of life seems as inscrutably remote to us as it has ever been. Even if we can generate in a laboratory some simplified organic molecules, we still have little notion of what makes up the life process.

Life, ever more abundant, diversified, and interdependent, dancing life is earth's most important story and its only product. It has been popular in Western civilization to assume that man is the goal of life, the crown of creation, the end for which all the rest is only a means. Much Judeo-Christian theology has shared in this popular assumption and its accompanying conclusion that only man is the child of God. Nature, thus reduced to a dispensable means, is only the backdrop to the big story of man. Worse yet, nature, to civilized man, seems unfriendly, even hostile, a foe to be conquered, a wild, uncontrolled thing to be made subject to man and civilized. As we shall soon see, this latter step really means substituting man's limited knowledge for the wisdom learned in two billion years of nature's process, binding the earth with concrete so it cannot support life and replacing complex life-supporting diversification with oversimplified man-made controls that allow entropy to start replacing life.

Cellular life (and all life is cellular) is very delicate; the conditions under which it can exist are restricted and have not changed appreciably since life appeared on earth. Cellular life requires the presence of nourishing liquid and only the "invention" of an incredible host of diverse ways of maintaining that liquid has allowed life to push itself to the limits of the biosphere, from the deserts to the poles, from the depths of the oceans to the upper reaches of the mountains, and with exceedingly clever and fiendishly expensive packaging and transporting of life-supporting ingredients from the biosphere, man has been able temporarily to leave it for a limited probe of space. But there are limits, and the nature and condition of these limits are most instructive. Never forget, life came forth in the sea, and it must take the sea with it wherever it goes in its unending quest.

In the warm ocean, salt and sun and moisture were readily available, but when life wanted to adventure, to reach out, it was necessary to build containers for maintaining the saline liquid and means, direct or indirect, for receiving energy from the sun. The most severe limit on life is this connection with energy from the sun. In our solar system, there is no other ultimate source of energy for life. Hence, every form of life is dependent upon it, and to continue must maintain a viable delivery system. Could the ancients of Egypt and elsewhere have understood this in some way now forgotten or mysterious to us? Is that why there are so many sun-god religions? Perhaps this understanding is behind the splendid mystery of Stonehenge near Salisbury in England, where a stone computer for predicting solstices and eclipses was laid out with astonishing accuracy.

However that may be, when life adventured to the land, it was necessary to build support systems to utilize the energy of the sun while maintaining the moisture and salt of the sea. All life is dependent on these two necessities. How can we best know and appreciate these beautiful support systems which life has developed, incredibly complex and diverse, yet as reliable as the sun?

Ian L. McHarg tells of a visit to the great architect, Louis Kahn, at a time when Kahn was designing an experimental environment.[1] The task was to discover how an astronaut might be sent to live in space or on the moon with a minimum of baggage. Kahn was attempting to solve this problem by providing a recirculating system, that is, a biological system. His original design called for a plywood capsule with a fluorescent light substituting for the sun, some air, water, some bacteria, and a man. In this proposed environment, the man breathes air and turns its oxygen into carbon dioxide; the algae in turn consume the carbon dioxide and return oxygen. Secondly, the man drinks water and expels urine which is returned to the water medium in which the algae and bacteria are located. Then the algae consume the water; it is transpired, condensed, and the man can again drink it. Thirdly, the man eats the algae, digests them and defecates. The decomposing bacteria change the feces into forms suitable for food for the algae, which can thus grow, providing more food for the man. This is a fully closed system except for the artificial sun and the export of some heat.

We know too little, McHarg reminds us, to keep such an experiment going for more than twenty-four hours, but its lessons are clear. Sun, photosynthesis, and recycling, all in a suitable temperature, are essentials for any form of life. This is the way the whole world works. Everything is connected to everything else, a first law of ecology. It is perhaps shocking to some to discover that man is a parasite in this scene. His contributions can be used, but they are not necessary as are the other processors, bacteria and algae. Man cannot synthesize the energy of the sun as do the plants, nor can he decompose waste products into usable material as do bacteria; the latter, of course, can and do use his wastes.

A closed system, essentially self-supporting, except for the sun, is called an ecosystem. There are two basic types, the terrestrial—a forest or grassland—and the open water aquatic system—a lake or sea. "Eco" as used here stands for ecology, a word derived from the Greek root *oikos,* meaning "house." Ecology is the study of the biology of environments, the structure and function of nature. An ecosystem is simply a term for nature, usually applied to a recognizable unit that is essentially integrated and largely self-supporting, and including the organisms and the non-living portions of the environment. The hypothetical system designed by Louis Kahn was an ecosystem.

There are two biotic components in any ecosystem: the one called the autotrophic, or self-nourishing, which is able to synthesize the light of the sun and simple inorganic substances into food, and the other called heterotrophic, or nourished by others, which decomposes the materials synthesized by the autotrophes into their simple constituents.

Ecologists recognize four components which comprise the ecosystem. First, the *abiotic substances,* the basic organic and inorganic compounds of the environment. Second, the *producers,* the autotrophic organisms. Third, the *consumers* or *macroconsumers,* heterotrophic organisms which utilize the products of the producers as food. Fourth, the *decomposers* or *microconsumers*, also heterotrophic organisms, but these break down the complex compounds of dead protoplasm, absorb some of the decomposition products and release substances usable by the producers.

If the above sounds too technical, consider again the two basic ecosystems, terrestrial and aquatic. In a grassland system, soil and air contain the basic compounds, such as phosphorus, oxygen, nitrogen, hydrogen, carbon, etc. The producers are plants; usually large-rooted plants such as trees comprise the majority, with additional plants such as shrubs and grass. The consumers are the insects, animals, and birds who feed directly on the plants, and the indirect consumers who feed on them. The decomposers are the bacteria, earthworms, and fungi of decay resident mostly in the soil. In an aquatic ecosystem the water and air contain the basic compounds. The producers are microscopic floating plants called phytoplankton. The consumers are the direct feeders who eat the phytoplankton and are called zooplankton; they are the most numerous creatures of the sea and provide the basic food for most of the sea's creatures. The decomposers are again the bacteria and fungi, but those belonging to the aquatic realm. It is important to grasp this fourfold realm of the ecosystem because no portion of it is unnecessary or superfluous, and man has neglected this cycle to his peril.

Man too easily forgets his intimate relation to his environment. His constant company with machines of late has led him to forget that he is neither bred, born, nor fed by machines, nor can they take care of his need for love and companionship along the road of life. The machine is at best a very dull-witted slave, and man stands rooted to the soil and sea from whence he came.

"It began as such things always begin—in the ooze of unnoticed swamps, in the darkness of eclipsed moons. It began with a gasp for air." [2] So Loren Eiseley tells the story of that primitive ancestor of man as it made its bid for life by climbing out of a drying swamp. The Snout, as Eiseley calls it, was one among many strange creatures of the bottom ooze, and from them to us, three hundred million years of time has unrolled. The world was a much less hospitable place then than it is now. The days brought incessant blasting heat, and frequent dust storms darkened the sun. The primitive plants, clustered only by the waters, left the land unprotected to be brutally eroded by the occasional torrents of rain.

On the oily surface of the pond, from time to time a snout thrust upward, took in air with a queer grunting inspiration, and swirled back to the bottom. The pond was doomed, the water was foul, and the oxygen almost gone, but the creature would not die. It could breathe air direct through a little accessory lung, and it could walk. In all that weird and lifeless landscape, it was the only thing that could. It walked rarely and under protest, but that was not surprising. The creature was a fish.[3]

But it was not just a fish. Something new was beginning, brought about perhaps, maybe selected by, the extremes of the tide and swamp flat. This strange creature, something like the walking catfish that has recently begun to trouble southern Florida, was making its first step toward becoming a land creature. But it was there in the swamp, says Eiseley, that something even more important began to happen behind the eyes of this air-gasping, flipper-walking oddity. "Perhaps there also among the rotting fish heads and blue, night-burning bog lights moved the eternal mystery, the careful finger of God. The increase was not much. It was two bubbles, two thin-walled little balloons at the end of the Snout's small brain. The cerebral hemisphere had appeared." [4]

These bubbles were the necessary invention to allow the brain tissue to be supplied with the oxygen which its ravenous appetite demanded. The bubble construction of their walls marks the difference between the higher creatures and the insects, whose brain development is solid and leads to elaborate instinct-bound patterns of behavior. Modern fishes, some reptiles, and all birds likewise have solid brains. The Snout chose a pattern of development which was to lead in the direction of a high order of consciousness.

So man's primitive ancestor, whose salt solution still dominates man's body, came forth from a tidal flat. Looking backward through three hundred million years somehow seems to tempt man to think that he is the final product at which earth life has aimed. Looking ahead, we see only idealized versions of ourselves dominating the solar system and extending ourselves via space travel multiple light years into the universe around us. But are we really the end product? Did the novas explode and create the elements just to lead to us? Did even earth undergo its birth pangs and the continents separate from the waters just on our behalf? The Genesis account does end with the Sabbath rest of God on the seventh day, but it does not imply that there was never to be an eighth day.

Life's ceaseless search to explicate itself into ever more complex, beautiful, and differentiated forms has not ended. A long look at the tidal swamp flat discloses experiments still under way. Who can say just now that the walking catfish is not the wave of the future, or is it perhaps the already well advanced porpoise? Without time travel or foreknowledge of the future, it is not possible to estimate or even guess which animal possesses the successful adaptive ability. Certainly the perils of the present which are the product of man—the threat of nuclear holocaust, noise, air, water, and land pollution, overpopulation, plus land and water misuse—give us no basis for optimism about man's future. More yet, this myopic egocentric concentration on man ignores the vast resources of Life which drives ever onward in its ceaseless search. Let us make no mistake, we are not the perfect image of Life, but only one of its manifold appearances and we may be a self-endangered species.

Man's brain, the source of his major distinction from other creatures, creates the ideas, or predilections, which fix the patterns of his social behavior. Ideas are the source of most of man's misery and joy; they are his most creative product and the source of his most dangerous illusions, for an idea is an image of "the way things are," the way the world really works. Such images govern the way we perceive and hence respond.

The dominant image that man has had of himself in Western civilization is *homo faber,* the crown of creation for which all else is mere stage or backdrop. *Homo faber,* man the maker and doer, man the scientist, technician, craftsman, man the master and maker of things; thus have we viewed ourselves. Further, Western science and technology, especially technology, with their underlying assumptions now dominate the world of man. Implicit within this framework is an assumption of perpetual progress. As this doctrine, for that is what it has become, has developed it has been linked to and dependent upon a certain pattern of Judeo-Christian teleology, not the only pattern, but for us the best known. This pattern of teleology views man as the purpose for which the rest of creation is made and more importantly as its master. The Bible is usually cited as the justification for this belief, the Genesis creation stories in particular, for there it is said of man alone that he was created in the image of God. And to man God said, "Be fruitful and multiply, and fill the earth and subdue it; and have dominion over the fish of the sea and over the birds of the air and over every living thing that moves upon the earth" (Gen. 1:28).

The words translated as "subdue" and "have dominion" are strong expressions, according to von Rad, the great German Old Testament scholar.[5] They mean, he says, that man is to have status as lord in the world, the sign of God's own sovereign authority, but only in order that man should uphold and enforce God's claims as Lord. Man is, then, merely God's representative; he does not have automatic authority. Further, as the next few verses of Genesis make clear, man's right does not include killing or slaughtering animals. The food for both man and animals is to be the plants of the earth. Later, man holds to the doctrine that he is to be the lord of creation, and gradually "forgets" that he is such only as the sign of God's Lordship, and that both he and the animals, those in whom dwells the "breath of life," are to have only plants for their food!

The second creation story of Genesis, though vastly different, gives much the same picture of man as lord under God. But immediately following it begins a series of stories of man's "sin" (alienation from God) and its effects. The essence of man's sin is his attempt to transcend his creaturely limitations, to "be like God." The end result was not at all what was expected, but a life of Sisyphus-like unending toil, involved in a hapless struggle with the power of evil and facing inescapable death. His alienation from God now permeates his whole nature, and his life is plagued with fear. Man who came from the soil is now alienated from it. No longer are its benign gifts the motherly basis of his whole life. Cast out of the paradisical garden, man finds even the soil cursed, and doubly so after he becomes the murderer of his own kind. Undeterred even by a "skin of the teeth" escape from the Flood, man rushes on in his mad course of history, building, dreaming of establishing permanently his obvious superiority with his technology.

Homo faber is in full sway as the Tower of Babel rises

to mark man's gigantic work of "civilization." The end to this program of godlikeness is brought about by man's inner alienation, brother against brother and tribe against tribe, symbolized by ruptured communications—"The Lord confused the language of all the earth" (Gen. 11:9). This story seems to mark the limit of God's patience, for it, unlike the preceding instances of the garden, Cain and Abel, the Flood, makes no promise of God's continuing presence. Are the nations to be allowed to go their own way? The confessional answer given in Gen., ch. 12, is the call of Abraham and God's declared intention to bless all the peoples of the earth through him.

Despite the fact that, for the Bible, the rest of creation is seemingly made of subsidiary importance to man, it is clear that at no point is the world conceived of as an entity set over against man. "Our current concept of 'world' was foreign to ancient Israel." [6] Further, it is of critical note that man is of the earth and intimately dependent upon it and only in a derived sense is he its lord, and then only as a sign of God's Lordship. Finally, man "falls" into alienation, first from God and then progressively from self, soil, and society. These "creation and fall" stories are designed to link the creation to the saving history of Israel which begins with Abraham, not to give a statement of the nature of man, nor even to declare him the crown of creation, the last for which the first was made.

Creation is not a thing which was formed "once upon a time," not a being, but a continuing event, an ongoing process. It can never be properly understood apart from the intention of God who works in and through creation. But man has gone a long way down the road which Martin Heidegger calls "forgetting of being." The meaning of the created world as God's creation has been forgotten; the world has become just a collection of things and processes which man may, if he is clever enough, turn to his advantage through science and technology. Forgotten are the hundreds of millions of years of experimentation through which the myriad forms of life came to be and learned to live in delicate balance in the biosphere. So to speak, nature has tried most of the things man is now experimenting with and found them destructive of life, as will be seen in the pages to come.

In the early church, both Eastern and Western, the created world was, for the most part, viewed as finite. According to Augustine, it was created out of nothing, at a given moment, by an act of God's free will. This view prevailed throughout the medieval period, in fact, up until the seventeenth century. Man, body and soul, is a created being and thus is part of creation. Augustine believed that God's Ideas are implanted in the creation. Matter is not mere stuff, but living potentiality awaiting the proper occasion to give effect to the Ideas of the divine mind and actualize itself in images which can be perceived through the senses (sensible experience). The soul is imbued with the divine light to become conscious of the Ideas as they are encountered through sensible experience. There is also revealed knowledge through church and Bible, which goes hand in hand with the truth that God is revealing through nature. In later ages this pattern shifts to a deliberate study of nature in an effort to understand God's mind. Finally, science and theology separate and the knowledge of nature is pursued as an end in itself.

Technology developed little during the many centuries between the golden period of Greece during the fifth century B.C. and the beginning of the fourteenth century, although there were some significant advances in agricultural methods. In addition, the medieval craft guilds guarded their processes as carefully as the Pentagon does its war plans and techniques. Hence, new techniques, even if discovered, were never popularized, but retained as local specialities. The theologically oriented scientific thinkers thus could benefit but little nor did they feel a need to, from technicians, and the latter looked only to their own kind of enlightenment. Not until science was secularized and the craft guilds were commercialized was this pattern to change. Science, which was once the desire to know of God through his creation, and was a labor of love, was to become the pursuit of knowledge for the sake of power. Technology was wedded to the emerging commercialism and became the handmaid of science in the service of profit.

In its foundations, modern science was still presuming the world to be a created order. It was the presumption of a God-given order manifest in nature that allowed the search for natural laws. But in another way, even in its origin, science broke with the Christian understanding of its day. Christianity, following the Bible, thought of the world in historic and finite terms. The time span of the world's existence is bounded by the Creation and Judgment Day; the world is finite with finite boundaries. God alone is infinite. Science gradually abandoned these limits and came to think of the universe as infinite in space, if not in time. C. F. von Weizsäcker in *The History of Nature* puts it very well: "Modern man thinks he can breathe freely only if his conquest of the world is no longer hindered by insurmountable limitations of his knowledge and his power." [7] He rejects the idea that there are any barriers between himself and the tree of knowledge.

The new notion of an infinite universe was given a religious foundation by transferring to it qualities previously reserved for God. Nicholas of Cusa saw in the world an image of God's infinity which passes our understanding. Newton thought of infinite space as the sensorium of God. As the years rolled by, the religious rationale was forgotten, but the doctrine of an infinite universe remained. Gradually, the understanding of the historic character of the world as the created arena of God's saving activity was transmuted into the thought that nature itself was historical through evolution. The purpose of evolution was to produce man, and now evolution was working out its purpose in man's history, i.e., man was truly the pinnacle of creation, glory to man the maker and master of things.

Today a huge problem has arisen, however; science has gradually disproved its most important presupposition, the infinity of nature. Any rigorous application of the second law of thermodynamics shows that the universe is finite in space and especially in time. Entropy cannot be denied. And, as von Weizsäcker notes, "the Second Law is not just any empirical law. In fact, it can be derived from principles so basic that it would be difficult to conceive the possibility of circumstances so different that the law would be no longer valid." [8] In fact, to abandon this law would require the assumption of a situation in which "the past does not consist of what has happened and is factual, and the future does not consist of what is to come and is possible."[9] We must give up the presupposition of science of infinite nature existing as such, of itself. We can no longer, then, look to the perpetual progress of natural evolution to give meaning and purpose to man's existence. Nor can man return to the faith of the Middle Ages like that held by Nicholas or Newton.

Although the details sketched above are not popularly

known, the conclusion of meaninglessness is widely felt. Modern man feels himself to be adrift in a mechanical universe which neither knows nor cares of his fate. Omnipotent time rolls on day by day, careless of the mortals who have thought themselves so much in control of affairs. Nihilism has pervaded much of the population of the developed nations. The ultimate outcome of approaching nature as a thing to be conquered, as something which could be known and against which man was free to act without love is that meaningless state called nihilism. Let us see how man has used this knowledge acquired without love.

What image was man to have of himself, his purpose, and destiny when the medieval myth of history as God's arena of salvation began to fade? At first, man seems to have combined two or more themes in Western civilization. He retained the idea of salvation, but began to look for evidences of it in his dealings with the natural world rather than in the sacraments and assurances of the church. Again, because the Christian religion formed the intellectual backdrop, this new idea was expressed in religious terms, but nonetheless a new and basically secularistic set of social, political, and economic ideas were being formed. It is beyond the scope of this work to do more than hint at them, but that much is necessary to understand the foundations of our consumption-obsessed society whose mute symbol of success is the ever-growing size of its garbage heap.

At the outset, the economic, political, and social theorists framed their theories within the context of Christian thought. When the Reformation began, economics was still a branch of ethics and ethics, a branch of theology. The propriety of economic and political schemes and practices was established by reference to theology. But more and more, religion came to be viewed as only one department within the whole social establishment and the others were to have their own proper basis for knowledge and value. And man? "From a spiritual being, who, in order to survive, must devote a reasonable attention to economic interest, man seems sometimes to have become an economic animal, who will be prudent, nevertheless, if he takes due precaution to assure his spiritual well-being." [10] It is but a small step from this dualism, which regards religion as basically unrelated to the institutions of society, to seeing religion as unrelated to life at all. Religion, as a purely private matter, which can have no voice in the public and corporate affairs of man, allows the rampant development of a society whose logical conclusion is nihilism and whose sole sense of direction is ever-increasing consumption. Thus, the god of economic growth is born.

To give even the devil his due, one cannot help being awed by the achievements of science and technology which have transformed the face of the material earth since the late seventeenth century. But, as Tawney has reminded us, if economic ambitions are good servants, they are, nonetheless, bad masters. Neither science, technology, nor economic ambition can really tell us for what the wheels turn. Uncritical worship of economic growth is unreason. The result is a world in which men seem to command a splendid mechanism which they can neither control nor fully use, and which threatens to destroy them with its misused and misjudged power. The mechanism narcotizes man with the illusion of progress wrested from the material environment by persons too dull of spirit to define the purpose to which its triumphs shall be applied.

Mankind has wrung nature's secrets of power from her and now wrangles over whom the power is to serve. No man can decry a wise economic efficiency, but as this book will show, when economic efficiency is made the primary goal, efficiency itself is destroyed. If economic growth is the primary goal, the final rule becomes unrestricted competition, but the necessary condition for any society is cooperation. The only basis of cooperation is a general agreement as to ends which are to be served and the criteria by which both ends and means are to be evaluated.

The question that the world's economic growth cultures have been unable to resolve is the comparative importance of economic interests versus other interests. In view of the finiteness of the earth's resources, how much material resources shall be sacrificed in this generation to expand education, to extend leisure, to improve housing, to provide military security, or to humanize working conditions? An adequate answer must be based on some conception of the requirements of human nature as a whole, of which economics is only a part. It was this conception, once provided in Western culture by Christianity, which is now lacking.

Capitalism came into being in a culture dominated by Christian values. Economic and political thinkers of the Middle Ages took it as a fundamental assumption that the ultimate standard of human institutions as well as individuals was the Christian religion. Hence, they attempted to shape all institutions and regulate all activities to aid man in the ultimate goal of life, viz., its relation to God. Society was organized functionally into classes and to each class specific rewards, or means of living, and rights were awarded. Each person was to receive the means appropriate to his station and must claim no more or his neighbor would go short and society would suffer. Each was to get what would maintain him in his function and no more. That this system had vices as well as virtues goes without saying. The point is that it was one way to organize society within the then ruling Christian insights. Society was held together by a system not dominated by economic self-interest, but by mutual though varied obligations.

Along with a system of social organization went a doctrine of economic ethics that was likewise dominated by Christian values. It is of no small note that the papacy, which was the greatest financial institution of the Middle Ages, was also probably the greatest violator of the economic ethics propounded by the church. It was this gradually worsening situation more than any other factor which led to the Reformation. Nonetheless, the church did propound, to meet the rapid growth of trade, of town life, and of a commercial economy, an eminently practical set of ethical principles. Their fundamental assumptions, however, are of more importance to us than their specific prescriptions; they were two: "That economic interests are subordinate to the real business of life, which is salvation; and that economic conduct is one aspect of personal conduct, upon which, as on other parts of it, the rules of morality are binding."[11] "At every turn, therefore, there are limits, restrictions, warnings against allowing economic interests to interfere with serious affairs." [12] Trade is legitimate, though hazardous to the welfare of the soul, and one must be sure that one carries it on for the benefit of the general public and takes only such profit as represents fair wages for one's labor. Private property is necessary because man is fallen, as a condescension to man's frailty, not because it is good in itself.

The general assumption about material goods underlying all of this is that economic desires, though legitimate, are inherently dangerous, and that their danger increases in direct proportion to the pecuniary interests associated with them.

> He who has enough to satisfy his needs, and nevertheless ceaselessly labors to acquire riches, either in order to obtain a higher social position, or that subsequently he may have enough to live without labor, or that his sons may become men of wealth and importance—all such are incited by a damnable avarice, sensuality, or pride.[13]

Nor were such ideas merely preached by the church; they formed the functioning ideas and were enacted into law by borough, manor, and national governments, including, in many places, public fixing of prices.

Despite the preachments, rules, laws, and general moral negativism, however, the idea of a commercialized society grew rapidly. Craft guilds, merchants, traders, bankers, financiers, and politicians, once grasped by the zeal for profit, quickly found ways to deal with their conscience. In this practice, of course, they found the example of the papacy, which was currently vying with state rulers for earthly power and glory, to be most helpful. None could exceed the papal powers in the rationalization of conscience.

Hence, by Martin Luther's century, a commercialized economy was well established. Luther, however, a man of rigorous conscience, searched the Bible carefully, and finding no warrant for capitalism, and avarice specifically condemned, tried to restore to society the simple Christian virtues, such as faith, hope, and charity, and dismissed the commercial society of his day as a lapse into paganism. He was repelled by the mechanisms which the church had developed to control commercial greed. God speaks to the individual soul, not through priests or human social institutions, but to the individual human heart alone. This radical individualism of the soul before God, guided by the Bible alone, made the whole apparatus of church, hierarchy, canon law, sacraments, and corporate worship irrelevant. All that society needed was for each man to love his neighbor as himself. Luther did not follow his logic to its conclusion, but later thinkers did and the whole medieval conception of the social order as an articulated organism of members contributing in their different degrees to a spiritual purpose was shattered. Secular interests, thus detached from a religious purpose, sought for a new master and found it in the profit motive. Later, Protestantism, following Luther, emptied religion of its social content and society of its soul by making religion an individual and purely spiritual affair.

The Swiss Reformers, led by John Calvin, took a wholly different approach to the problem. Calvinism did not try to turn back the clock, but assumed the existence of a commercial society and proceeded to expound a Christian ethic to govern it. Their motif was that persons who hold to the gospel will prove themselves Christians by holiness of life. The enemy is not the accumulation of riches, but their misuse for self-indulgence or ostentation. The ideal is a society that seeks wealth in the disciplined fashion of men thus devoted to the service of God. Although accepting trade and banking as normal, Calvin forged a rigorous ethic for their control. Both individuals and the social order exist and work to the glory of God; that is their purpose. Hence, both need a discipline to keep

them so operating that the society can truly be called a
"Kingdom of Christ."

The dual thrusts of Calvinism were: Its insistence on
personal responsibility achieved through discipline and
asceticism, and the drive to Christianize the entire social
order. In Calvin's Geneva, the individualism was controlled by a rigorous discipline, with the church setting
rules and policies that the state enforced on the whole
social order. In England, however, the upper classes took
the individualism and abstained from the necessary discipline of the social order. *Laissez faire* in commercial dealings could not be farther from any position than from that
of Calvinism, which in such dealings consciously chose
authority over freedom as the better part of both wisdom
and righteousness.

There was an enthusiastic attempt by divines and
princes of the Church of England to bring into being a
social order disciplined to the glory of God, but they
lacked the wisdom and ingenuity of Calvin in Geneva.
Their major enemy was an idea more powerful in its appeal to the desires of man than the reward of religion
which the divines promised. That idea was that the individual is to be the unquestioned master of what he owns,
and may, within legally established limits, exploit it to his
monetary advantage without regard to its present or future
effect on the well-being of his neighbors and without
answer to any higher authority. This is the theory of private property. It appealed particularly to the English
landowners, the manorial lords, who set about populariz-
ing and defending it with vigor, since it strengthened their
rights and mitigated their responsibilities.

Against the individualistic commercial tide, the medieval social theory still held by the leaders of the Church of

England could not hold sway. It was but a voice from the past. Economic interests were soon appealing to the political theory of John Locke, which purported to prove that the state which interferes with property and business destroys its own title to existence. In a tour de force reversal, natural law was then taken to be not the will of God found in the world but human desires—hence, the sanctity of private property and free play for self-interest. Economics was effectively divorced from religion, because religion, presented as medieval social theory, had proved itself irrelevant.

Into this desultory scene strode the violent and vigorous movement known as Puritanism. Driven by the heaven-seeking piety of Bunyan, Fox, Milton, and Cromwell, the Puritan movement generated unprecedented social power. Its strong emphasis on individual responsibility and individual salvation appealed to those who had achieved economic independence and education, in short, those who had most benefited from private property, the commercial classes. But it appealed not as a license for economic libertarianism, but as a godly discipline of salvation well suited to free men of property or business vocations, and it imposed a strict ethic on economic affairs much like Calvin's in Geneva.

Nonetheless, as with Geneva, what began as strict religious control ended in utilitarian individualism. Puritanism, like Luther, broke from the "social organism" concept of society through its emphasis on individual salvation by personal faith. Neither conduct nor action can attain God's grace; it is a gift. But conduct and action can and do prove that one is God's chosen, and it is individual action! Riches are the blessing awarded to him who has responded to God's grace with energy, sobriety, and zeal.

The theory was self-discipline, but the result was *laissez faire*.

It was not long until the profit motive itself was duly baptized as a Christian duty and success in business seemed almost a sure sign of spiritual grace. Thus was fully laid the religious foundation for Adam Smith, who assumed that God had so made the world that a happy harmony existed between the needs of society and the self-interest of the individual. The worship of production, ever greater production, became hallowed by the identification of labor and enterprise with the service of God. Even consumption was hallowed because it led to ever greater productive energies. With these twin goals, at first religiously hallowed, but later so firmly entrenched that they could be detached fully from religion, the modern epic of capitalistic technological man was on its way. Man was freed to ravish the earth with a clear conscience, so long as it made a personal profit.

It will be the task of the remainder of this book to show that what makes bad theological sense also makes for human destruction and perhaps human extermination. The ideology of an ever-expanding economic growth is the etiology of cancer.

2

POPULATION,
PROGRESS, AND PROFIT

There are numerous instances in world history in which a society has reached what was to it a desired size and has then found a means to stabilize itself. One of the South Pacific tribes invented a primitive intrauterine device. Further, although they readily tolerate premarital intercourse, a girl whose sexual exploits result in pregnancy is socially ostracized and no longer marriageable.

The Irish potato famine of 1845 to 1850 is a classic illustration of the theory of Malthus: "If the only check on the growth of population is starvation and misery, then no matter how favorable the environment or how advanced the technology, the population will grow until it is miserable and starves." In 1700, Ireland had a population of some two million, just about balanced with food production. Then from the New World came the potato, making more food available. There were no social bars to early marriage and childbirth, and population began to grow rapidly. By 1846, population had reached eight and a half million people living at the edge of misery in poverty. Then came the potato blight, which destroyed the crop year after year. During that time two million people starved to death and two million emigrated. Rigid morals, late marriages, and emigration have resulted in a stable population.

Why is man not now limiting his population appropriately, even in those sections of the world where increase obviously means immediately increased starvation and misery? In mankind's brief history, there have been probably two other periods of rapid increase in population. The first of these occurred after the first development of tools to aid in hunting and food-gathering. The second occurred after the development of agriculture some ten thousand years ago. The present explosive growth began after the scientific-industrial-commercial revolution of the seventeenth century, but has continued to increase in rate up to the present time. The two previous periods of growth seem to have been spurred by increasing availability of food and were curbed as soon as the population reached a reasonable relation to food supply, probably well below the starvation level. This natural limitation seems not to be working, and we seek to discover why it is not.

Much has been made of the Genesis admonition to man to "multiply and subdue the earth" as a prime source of the present population problem. Although it certainly must share some of the blame as a concept which has outlived its usefulness so long that it has become a hazard, it is clear that there are other perhaps more profound causes. First, it is to be noted that man, apart from the Judeo-Christian heritage, seems to have an equal drive to increase his kind. It seems probable that the foremost cause of large families in the history of the world is the simple utility of offspring. They serve as additional helpers in a world of work, and as old-age insurance in a world with little old-age security. Fertility is an ancient goddess whose worship was not unrelated to her utility.

The fertility cults of the ancient Near East were not only not adopted into Christianity but were specifically proscribed for Israelites and bitterly opposed by the prophets. There was a strongly polemical attitude toward the deification of sex, and it was carefully excluded from all worship events. There was to be no thought of salvation through procreation. Nonetheless, fertility of man, animals, and land were considered a blessing given by God to his faithful people. This latter teaching is transcended, or even denied, by Jesus in his statement that God sends his sun and rain alike to the just and the unjust. There is no material blessing for faith in God. Nor was Israel allowed to forget that the land belonged to God alone; people were only "strangers and sojourners" who had use of the land under God's Lordship.

Secondly, the present population surge did not begin until the processes of exchanging Christian goals for secularistic goals, as described in Chapter 1, had been under way for several hundred years. Thus it seems quite dubious to attach the blame to the Judeo-Christian heritage. The really new factors beginning in the seventeenth century are not attributable to Christianity.

As mentioned above, the population problem is not confined to nations predominantly Judeo-Christian in tradition. Those nations of the world least influenced and dominated by Christianity are today struggling with the problem of overpopulation. India, which is overwhelmingly Hindu, is perhaps the clearest example. Japan, likewise, on whose arable land the density of population is among the highest in the world, has been dominantly Shinto, with some Buddhist adherents. In recent history, Japan's population has been kept under control largely through abortion.

The basic ideological elements underlying the present

population explosion would seem to be found in the cultural developments unique to our period. The new ideological factors are those still dominating our scientific-technological-commercial culture. Its foremost principle is the conviction that *growth is always good.* This idea stems basically from the economic goals of the commercialized civilization and the assumption of endless evolution with man himself leading the way and scientific technology providing the means. Our modern "growth" societies, with their expectation of an ever-increasing standard of living, are the logical outcome.

The developments of technology were quickly applied to farming with a consequent increase in available food. An article in *Lancet,* a British medical journal of considerable world renown,[14] concludes that the rapid rise in population beginning in the eighteenth century, and particularly evident in the nineteenth, was due primarily to a reduction of death by disease. This reduction was not so much a result of either healthier conditions or medicine, but rather solely because of improved nutrition resulting from industrialization. No one can denounce or regret this improvement. The puzzle is, Why did not man begin to apply medicine to birth control as he did effectively to death control in the early twentieth century? The only answer that can make sense is that he wanted an ever-increasing population. Why?

Advancing commercial needs and the extension of the geographic horizon creating a feeling of spaciousness in the world had already pushed man to press out from Europe into the other continents where he could easily believe that there was a seemingly endless new space to inhabit. Improving transportation and navigation made immigration an attractive prospect. Further, the increased number of ships could bring in food to needy areas. These factors, combined with the dissolution of any sense of stewardship responsibilities for the creation, allowed man to use the earth in any way it pleased him and recklessly to extend his own number, believing that he was actually adding to his potential prosperity. Still today, the business leaders of the United States seem to regard an increasing population as a welcome guaranteed increase in their market.

Gradually, but consistently, man has been moving farther and farther away from the soil in terms of his vocations, his locations, and his avocations. As the movement from rural areas to the city, from farming to factories, from involvement to spectator sports and mechanized recreation has progressed, man has lost touch with his natural rootages. This gradual divorce from nature and constant life with the machine and its products have led man to conceive his ideal environment as an air-conditioned, plush-carpeted, fluorescent-lighted paradise, equipped with a self-activating automat to provide synthetic food on demand, a tiled swimming pool full of distilled water, wall-to-wall stereo plus television, with no clouds, rain, sun, germs, dirt, animals, or birds (except highbred pets), and no greenery other than plastic imitations needing no care, nothing wild, nothing uncontrolled—in short, nothing natural.

Is it not possible that man in his dreams of artificial utopias is planning an environment in which he cannot live? Many experiments with other species suggest that such is indeed the case. An experiment by Roscoe Spencer and his colleagues with single-celled organisms revealed that a seemingly perfect environment was less desirable from the standpoint of species survival than one in which the individuals were not protected. In fact, all efforts to keep paramecia populations alive in an "ideal" environment resulted in the death of the populations within a few years, whereas populations enduring ordinary laboratory conditions can be kept alive indefinitely.[15] The same is true of other simple organisms, and the general conclusion is that there is a complementarity between "population erosion" and "population vigor" and between the continuity of the species and the inevitable death of the individual. The specific mechanism involved seems to reflect genetical health and sickness. The gene pool, apparently, does not respond favorably to "ideal" environments.

This divorce from the soil is part and parcel of man's "forgetting of being" which was noted in Chapter 1. Some ecological writers regret the abolition of animism by the prophets and apostles of the Judeo-Christian lineage. Lynn White, for example, writes: "By destroying pagan animism, Christianity made it possible to exploit nature in a mood of indifference to the feelings of natural objects." [16] And he believes that Governor Reagan of California spoke for the Christian tradition when he allegedly said, "When you've seen one redwood tree, you've seen them all." Despite the fact that, especially of late, some alleged Christians and even theologians have spoken and thought this way, it is not a fair or balanced representation of either Biblical teaching or a majority of Christian tradition. That the church has willingly approved the economic-growth culture for many decades now was shown in Chapter 1, but that this is a gross error and departure from its proper faith this book will demonstrate.

The Israelite prophets combated the animism of the other local religions, not in order to desacralize nature, but to make it clear that those alleged divinities were impotent idols. The one true God was Yahweh and the created order was his. It was not only not necessary to do business with the nature spirits, but was superstitious, a worship of imaginary gods. Harvey Cox, in *The Secular City*, has argued that the prophets' disenchantment of nature made modern science possible. It is crucial to note, however, that he interprets disenchantment to mean turning nature into an object, a thing which is not a god, but neither is it a living entity to which man can have a filial relationship.

Cox jumps directly from animism to the modern view of nature and assumes that this is the step made by the prophets. They were removing the false spirits from nature, true, but they did not teach that Yahweh could be perceived only in history and not in nature, nor, as has been shown earlier, did they reduce nature to a thing subject to man's whimsical dominion.

No distinction is made by the Old Testament between the world of history and the world of nature.[17] Man's rule was derived from Yahweh, who retained title to the whole creation. Cox makes the same kind of leap in the realms of politics, history, and values, and in each case assigns a modern secularistic view to the Biblical writers which was beyond their imagining. They intended rigorously to combat and eliminate the worship of false, imaginary gods, but only in order to replace them with Yahweh, *never* in order to replace them with man in godless time, opposed by a nature bereft of God. Our abstract secularist concepts of time, history, nature, politics, and values all belong exclusively to that modern way of thinking which has developed largely since the seventeenth century and from which any God concept has been carefully eviscerated.[18]

We need to recover and restate an idea suggested by the Old Testament and specifically taught by many world religions, that God is present and can be encountered in nature. The Old Testament Wisdom Literature (Job, Proverbs, Ecclesiastes, etc.) teaches that there is a deeply hidden order in all things and events. This is so because Yahweh creates with his Wisdom, which is thus continually being made manifest. The wise man seeks for this Wisdom in the creation (i.e., for us, nature and history). "Wisdom is now understood as the divine call to men, and therefore as the mediator of revelation: it is the great teacher of all the nations and of Israel in particular. . . . [It] is the divine principle bestowed upon the world at Creation." [19] This Wisdom of Yahweh calls man to life and salvation and is the same word which he made use of as a plan in his original act of creation.[20] And this call of Wisdom comes in ordinary life, quite apart from overtly religious events. It is, in the later portions of the Wisdom writings, not to be learned by man by his observation of history as natural processes. God's Wisdom always transcends man's knowledge, but it calls to man through the creation, through life itself.

With this concept we come very close to the idea of the Logos (the creating word or reason) of God which is found in the Prologue to the Gospel of John. It is the Logos by which God creates and it is the Logos which is present in flesh in Jesus. Raymond Brown in his recent and excellent commentary, *The Gospel According to John*, indicates that John, in presenting Jesus as an incarnate revelation who offers men light and truth, "has capitalized on an identification of Jesus with personified divine Wisdom as described in the Old Testament." [21] Much of later Christianity and most contemporary Christianity seem to have lost track of this connection between the Logos in Jesus and the Old Testament understanding of Wisdom; this forms another link in man's "forgetting of being," losing his close tie to creation and dwelling in the world of theoretical ideas. It is this latter against which the later Wisdom writings were specifically directed. They saw man's greatest peril as an overevaluation of his own knowledge and reason to the exclusion of God's Wisdom. The latter was termed *Sapientia* in Latin, and in medieval theology the knowledge given by revelation was called *sapientia* as contrasted with what man learned by reason and experience, called *scientia.* Thus, in becoming scientific, man ceased to be *homo sapiens,* the wise. He became *homo faber,* technological man.

Because man has lost his sense of connection with creation and has severed his cultural adventure from God, the only place to turn for meaning is to himself. If man is the end product of evolution and the only guarantor of continuing progress, and if the major meaning of culture is its ability to produce and consume, then more people are an unqualified blessing.

Rather than humility about his powers, what came to dominate the thought of man was the idea of indefinite progress coupled with the dream of the infinite perfectibility of man. Add to these the unleashing of greed brought on by the experience of the endless frontier and you have the prescription for raping the countryside for profit, proliferating the ever more complex and destructive technological society, cloaked with the naïve assumption that progress toward happiness will be the inevitable result.

The result of man's pride in his science and technology and his neglect of Wisdom has actually been a serious deterioration of the quality and possibility of life. He has

paved over the land, stripped the forests, and left the soil
naked for erosion. He has overplowed and overplanted the
once fertile soil until it has to be poisoned with overfertili-
zation to continue its yields. Dams have destroyed the
beauty of natural valleys and inundated priceless bottom-
lands—dams made necessary by stripping forests and
plowing up grasslands to farm marginal soil, or dams
made necessary by the need to irrigate new land to replace
the destroyed soils, or by the galloping technology with its
merciless demands for power. Rivers have been polluted
by bad farming technology prompted by greed, and industrial and domestic waste, and there is a growing water
shortage. Finally, the concept of the endless Frontier and
the idea of Progress have led to an ever-increasing rate of
depletion of all resources by our poliferating rate of consumption and expanding technology. In the chapters
ahead, a closer look will be had at the pressures brought
about on the environment resulting from population
growth and the proliferation of technology.

The power of two factors in lulling man to sleep, so that
the environment about him has deteriorated almost beyond recognition, can scarcely be overestimated. Those
factors are the *idea of Progress* and the *Frontier experience* from A.D. 1500 to A.D. 1900. The two are interre-
lated with one another and with the decisive break from
religion which was described earlier. That break had already begun when the idea of Progress began its development. Francis Bacon gave considerable impetus to this
development by declaring frankly that the purpose of his
work was to advance the "happiness of mankind" here on
earth by using science to endow "human life with new
inventions and riches." Previously, the goal of science was
deemed to be speculative satisfaction, knowledge for its

own sake. Bacon was convinced that science must be crassly practical. Looking at history, Bacon thought he was able to show that where contemplation and doctrinal science began, practical results ceased. The proper end of science, he said, was realized only as it extended the dominion of man over nature, thus increasing his comfort and happiness.

This stance of Bacon's had great influence over the scientific community and on the general populace. It was, by implication, a sharp break with the whole medieval understanding, by teaching that happiness on earth was an end worthy of pursuit for its own sake and that man could act in concert to obtain it. Although at the outset the meaning of happiness was not well defined, it soon became generally accepted that material welfare was a major component of it. Science, government, and, of course, commerce, all quickly made themselves faithful servants, at least in name, of the material welfare of mankind, while more often serving primarily themselves.

The developments above occurred at about the same time that the New World was being opened to full exploration and settlement. It is difficult to overstate the importance of this event in human history, particularly the history of the developed nations of the Western world. Prior to A.D. 1500, the known world, Europe, was fully explored, developed, and populated. Its population density was fairly stable, except for devastations such as the Black Plague, at about twenty-seven people per square mile. By 1650, the rapid discovery of new lands had added so much territory for settlement that when included they reduced the density to five persons per square mile. As was noted in Chapter 1, the societies of Europe were organized along class lines and were static; there was almost no social mobility. There was no idea of Progress. Suddenly, all of that changed. Just as man began to focus on his earthly material-based happiness, vast amounts of land, wealth, and food and clothing stuff appeared like manna from heaven; the Great Frontier opened. The Boom that was to last for three centuries had begun.

Hitherto, man had lived within the secure structure of civilization, and to it he looked for values, protection, and reward for his efforts. On the frontier all of these functions of civilization were absent. Everything was up to the individual. If there were to be any rewards, they had to be seized; there was no one to give or approve of their taking. From this situation new values began to emerge—freedom, independence, individual action, aggressiveness, courage, and ingenuity became the valued virtues of the new order. These were the virtues because in a frontier these characteristics resulted in maximizing material possessions. And just as society neither controlled nor assisted, so nature resisted, but only passively. There was no punishment for aggressive attack on nature and often much reward, so that the rape of natural resources became the rule of the day. In defense of this ruthless taking, one can only note that man was long starved, little controlled, and that natural abundance seemed literally inexhaustible.

The net result of this state of affairs was the emergence of what might be termed the native American religion, *work*. This culture has, until recently, lacked greatly in appreciation or practice of art, literature, drama, philosophy, and theology, nor could it appreciate gracious living. Frontier man went in for work because in his situation it paid off in the immediate rewards he wanted. The foremost apostle and popularizer of this new religion was Benjamin Franklin. In his *Poor Richard's Almanack*, he literally sold the nation on his view of the unadulterated rewards of hard, unremitting work. Not even the Bible had made a greater mark on the operating character of a people. This devotion to work, which began as a necessity, soon became the most popular creed of America and a principal article of economic faith, contrary to an aristocratic Europe where the work ethic was considered vulgar. Loafers there were, of course, but they received few rewards and no plaudits on the frontier.

The Frontier, however, was producing its effects on Europe also. We can scarcely imagine the intellectual impact made by the opening of new lands and the vast flow of goods which came to Europe from them. In France, the study of economics had arisen and grown to importance as man focused on his material welfare as a worthy goal. The physiocrats assumed that the proper end of the social order was earthly happiness for its members and that such was the sole purpose of government. This happiness they conceived in almost totally material terms. As Mercier de la Rivere describes it, "Humanly speaking, the greatest happiness possible for us consists in the greatest possible abundance of objects suitable to our enjoyment and in the greatest liberty to profit by them." [22]

Rivere further taught that liberty was doubly necessary, both to enjoy the objects and to produce them in abundance, since liberty stimulates human efforts. To this package he added the climax, another condition of material welfare, the multiplication of the human race to ensure many workers and consumers. For Rivere, liberty meant freedom to own, and use as one pleased, private property. Government's chief function was to protect property and ensure complete freedom for private enterprise to exploit the resources of the earth. All would be well if trade and industry were allowed to follow their natural inclinations. Note that this idea of liberty, destined to be so powerful, is purely economic. Bury states that neither the French philosophers nor the economists of that day had any just conception of political liberty.[23]

In England, Adam Smith was in wholehearted agreement with the French economists. He firmly believed in an abundance of material objects as contributing to the civilization and happiness of mankind. Free operation of traders and manufacturers, of commerce of any kind, was to the greatest advantage of all. Smith believed this idea represented a natural law just as fixed by God as Newton's physical laws of gravitation. Was he right?

Walter Prescott Webb, in his revolutionary work *The Great Frontier,* from which much of the above has been drawn, indicates that Smith's ideas of *laissez faire* had been practiced for a century by the frontiersmen before Smith enunciated them. Further, he argues, Smith's theories must be viewed against the effects which the Frontier had on England's economy, for only under those conditions does that theory make sense. England and Spain were the largest owners of the new frontier. This frontier represented a vast body of wealth now available in great disproportion to the small population of England. The condition that Adam Smith analyzed, then, was one of superabundant wealth ready for the taking. It is Webb's conviction that "free trade and *laissez faire* cannot exist in extreme form except in situations where wealth, real or potential, is abundant in proportion to population." [24] It was the Great Frontier which gave validity to Smith's major thesis, that all restrictions could and should be removed from the individual in search of wealth. His thesis, says Webb, was valid then and for a century to come, because those conditions lasted for a century, but such conditions were abnormal and temporally limited. Many passages from Smith's work are cited by Webb which show clearly that he was conscious that he wrote with the wealth of the frontier in mind as the condition for the system of society which he proposed. This condition, however, seems to have been little noted by those who popularized Smith's economic theories.

Also little noticed were two other factors in his theories. First, the purpose of the free market is to allow the market mechanism to work. Government, thus, should not put restraints on imports or exports, should not shelter industry from domestic or foreign competition and, of course, should not spend money on unproductive ends. But the great enemy of the free market, according to Smith, is not government; it is monopoly. "People of the same trade seldom meet together, but the conversation ends in a conspiracy against the public, or in some diversion to raise prices." It is surprising indeed that Smith, who warned against the grasping industrialists who "generally have an interest to deceive and even to oppress the public," soon became their patron saint. And even today, in ignorance of his actual thought, he is believed to be a conservative economist, "whereas in fact," writes Robert Heilbroner, "he was more avowedly hostile to the *motives* of businessmen than most New Deal economists." [25]

The other too often ignored condition of *laissez faire* presumed by Smith, but even more by his followers in America, has to do with their understanding of man, God, and society. Man is viewed as weak and imperfect, sinful and selfish, whereas, writes Bowen, society "is a complex and delicate machine, the real Author and Governor of which is divine." "God turneth their selfishness to good;

and ends which could not be accomplished by the greatest
sagacity, the most enlightened and disinterested public
spirit, and the most strenuous exertion of human legislators and governors, are effected directly and incessantly,
even through the ignorance, the willfulness, and the
avarice of man." [26] As has been noted, the wealth of the
frontier provided the necessary, but unnoticed, condition
for the seeming success of this belief. Also, as has been
noted, more secular minds were quick to forget the assumptions relating to the power of God and the weakness
of man in the success of this system. The secular assumptions that were equally dependent upon the frontier for
their apparent correctness were of the perfectibility of
man, the notion that heaven is really on earth, though in
the future, and the centrality of man in the scheme of
things.

The major block to full acceptance and dominance of
the idea of Progress as the principal natural law of society
was the remaining Christian conviction of original sin and
the concomitant biological concept of the fixity of the species. The Enlightenment had virtually knocked out original sin and substituted the infinite perfectibility of man;
now the theory of evolution was to provide the elimination
of the fixity of the species. Yet, at the same time, if taken
seriously, as some Christian leaders of the day perceived,
evolution took from man his remaining glory as a rational
being especially created to be the lord of the earth. Scientifically, evolution did not necessarily mean the progress of
the world to a goal desired for man, and it has been inter-
preted both to guarantee the end of man and to guarantee
the steady improvement of his condition. Those who
wanted to develop the idea of Progress with evolution as
its base tried to show that social life obeys the same laws

of evolution as nature and that this process involves an increase of happiness.

Herbert Spencer became the principal architect of the "Progress through evolution" position. It is not an overstatement to say that he was a rabid optimist. "The ultimate development of the ideal man is logically certain—as certain as any conclusion in which we place the most implicit faith; for instance, that all men will die." Progress, he believed, was not an accident, or a possibility, but a necessity. He grounded his conviction on the theological assertion that the ultimate purpose of the creation was to produce the greatest amount of happiness among men. Mankind is the true purpose of the creation and will evolve to be able to enjoy his life to the maximum. For this to be possible, man must evolve so that he will not interfere with the power of others to enjoy their lives to the maximum. At the outset, Spencer assumed the work of a benign Deity, but gradually shifted to an Unknowable existing behind all the perceptible material forces bringing into being the ends of a gigantic plan.

Spencer's ideas found a ready audience in the Western world, and Progress became a widely accepted article of faith. Along with this new dogma of faith in human progress in lieu of celestial rewards of the separate soul went a new ethical principle, consideration for posterity. If heaven is to come on earth in the future, then life now may be viewed either as a prelude to the future or as a preparation for the future. In either case, it has little immediate value. The full weight of this consideration has seldom been faced resolutely and it has instead resulted in the typical American parent who lives "for the kids." The logical conclusions of this futuristic orientation is further evaded by foreshortening the indefinite future to a better day tomorrow which can be reasonably expected within one's own lifetime.

The concept of the endless Frontier and indefinite Progress became intricately intertwined in the thoughts and assumptions of man, so that he has gone gaily onward raping the countryside for profit, proliferating his endless technological society naïvely, assuming that progress toward happiness must be the net result.

Some rather significant and far-reaching changes in man's theological understanding resulted from the idea of Progress and the seemingly endless Frontier. The ultimate purpose of man's life is no longer salvation, especially as represented by the hope of heaven; it is, rather, a future utopia consisting, in the main, of material welfare. Progress toward this utopia is continual and is guaranteed. For the secularists, this guarantee is the process of evolution and the natural abundance of the world, coupled with man's infinite perfectibility. For the religious, even though man is weak, God works through the processes of society to guarantee progress. There are no limits on man's ability to know through his reason. Science is organized reason, and man is clearly on the way to final knowledge; it is just a matter of time until the limited circle of knowledge will be filled in.

At the turn of the century, bright young men were discouraged from studying physics because all the basic knowledge had been learned and only mopping-up teams were required. This was just before the Curies discovered radium and Einstein promulgated his theory of relativity. Finally, although man is usually thought of as natural, he is the last and best product of nature and is moving to his ultimate destiny of perfection. The rest of nature is clearly to be subservient to man and his wants; it has no meaning in and of itself.

There is here a strange mixture of secularism and naïve trust in a beneficent deity. More and more, however, the deity is squeezed out or made automatic, e.g., providence is translated into natural or historical processes. What critique can be made of these beliefs from the viewpoint of Biblical faith? Certainly the Old Testament prophets who fought assiduously against the materialism of the worshipers of Baals, the Canaanite deities, would have lashed out against this modern materialism as a new idolatry. Nor can one imagine its getting much approbation from the Nazarene who taught men to seek first the Kingdom of God, and who said, "How hard it will be for those who have riches to enter the kingdom of God" (Mark 10:23). It is totally opposite to the wisdom of the apostle Paul in his letter to Timothy, a young pastor, which says, "Those who desire to be rich fall into temptation, into a snare, into many senseless and hurtful desires that plunge men into ruin and destruction" (I Tim. 6:9).

As for man's perfectibility, either by his own work or naturally by evolution, such an idea is utterly foreign to the Bible. There is no presumption of progress, nor could any value be given to such an idea, for the meaning of a person's life is in its relationship to God, not in the wealth of one's possessions, social position or prestige, power or knowledge, race, nation, sex, or other such characteristic. Nor is it the pious who are blessed, but the poor in spirit.

For the modern world, the mechanism by which progress occurs or by which abundance is to be gained is more and more presumed to be science and its practical right hand, technology. The faith that man had at the end of the nineteenth century was firmly vested in himself, his reason and his inventions. It did not seem to occur to many to question this faith on theological grounds, although the old adage "Pride goeth before a fall" was cer-

tainly not archaic yet. The Biblical background for this
adage is considerably more profound than the adage. It
includes the idea, similar to the Greek warning about arrogance, that undue self-confidence is like a set of blind-
ers; it causes one not to see a considerable portion of
reality, especially reality pertaining to one's own preju-
dices, faults, or weaknesses. In the New Testament, this
kind of tunnel vision is termed hypocrisy, a Greek word
meaning in literal translation, "under critical," i.e., not
self-critical. The later Wisdom Literature is particularly
apprehensive about man's pride with respect to his reason
or knowledge. Thinking oneself wise is the hallmark of the
fool who no longer listens for the Wisdom of God, but
trusts in himself. "Have you observed the man who thinks
he is wise? There is more hope for a stupid fool than for
him!" (The Anchor Bible, Prov. 26:12.) "He who relies
on his own ideas is a fool: It is the one who lives by
wisdom who survives." (The Anchor Bible, Prov. 28:26.)

Human knowledge, reason, action, are seen to be
bounded by an inscrutably mysterious void which they can
neither finally encompass nor control. The Wisdom writers
are the source of the aphorism "Man proposes, God dis-
poses." In Prov. 19:21, it reads, "Many are the plans in a
man's mind, but the Lord's will determines how things
will turn out" (The Anchor Bible). This is not a tragic
vision of man, but an honest facing of the limitations
which encompass human life. Nor does it, contrary to the
Greeks, presume a hidden Nemesis, a retributive god who
resents man, seeks vengeance, and limits man; it is simply
that man's knowledge and action are feeble indeed compared to the incalculable powers and inscrutable plans of
Yahweh. Wisdom calls man to trust in Yahweh. It calls
man to humility.

Post-World War II industrialized man is the epitome of all that is opposite to humility, and appears completely lacking in the knowledge of what is Biblically understood as living by Wisdom. He who had broken the secret of the atom stood at the brink of what appeared to be a dazzling new frontier. Utopia was in sight; the work-free, push-button world was just around the corner; the limits of space would be conquered; modern medicine would create a disease-free population; the chemical industry would shower on this most blessed of all creatures fabrics and plastics which would revolutionize living; the military would become invincible with awesome new weapons and transport; automobiles would be longer, faster, and more powerful; electric power and household appliances would practically eliminate housework and free housewives from manual drudgery; industrialized agriculture promised an abundance of food for a hungry world.

Some of the dream was realized by the middle of the century and the space program not only revolutionized communication, it actually succeeded in having a man on the moon before 1970. There are bigger and faster cars, and household appliances have greatly alleviated some kinds of drudgery. Miracle fabrics and plastics have contributed their share to the cultural revolution. But somewhere, somehow, the great industrial utopian dream began to look more like a nightmare. Unrest throughout the world has manifested itself in wars and revolutions, the world is still one half hungry, and the population continues to grow at an alarming rate. The technological revolution has begun to place demands on the creation that are running up debts mankind can ill afford to pay. The Great Frontier days—first space, then science—are coming to a screeching halt, and man is discovering all too rapidly, although perhaps not soon enough, that nature is neither passive nor conducive to aggressive conquest. In fact, nature has in many frightening ways revealed that she has inexorable laws which will be disobeyed at life's peril.

Industrial utopian promises have turned into threatening headlines which warn that mankind will be lucky to greet the twenty-first century firsthand, no matter what he does. Man has become, along with one thousand other species, an endangered species. The frail biosphere housing terrestrial life has revealed that it is neither entertained by nor tolerant of *homo faber*'s industrial drama. The enterprise of simple animals and primitive people is much more to its taste. Suddenly, many thoughtful, intelligent, and alarmed people have discovered that the industrial revolution has turned its cannons around and they are pointing squarely at mankind and life itself. Man's reckless exploitation of earth and its resources has worn out his welcome. Water, air, and soil all threaten to break down, eliminating life as we know it, and the system on which the creation is based is one that man is incapable of repairing. No fresh supply of water or air can be imported to bolster the poisoned and dwindling supplies. There is only so much soil; once poisoned or washed away, it seems highly unlikely that man will discover a speed-up process of producing even as much as an inch of topsoil which took nature five hundred years to produce.

To turn from the exploitation of the earth to its nurture, however, which is clearly called for, will be to overthrow the gods of population, progress, and profit. To suggest that such a reversal of modern industrial philosophy is vital, if man is to survive, is to question the basic premises, assumptions, and goals on which that philosophy is based. It is the conclusion of this book that this philosophy must not merely be questioned, but abandoned entirely. It is rapidly becoming all too apparent that instead of man's being the ultimate product of creation, there is no such thing as a "human ecology" as opposed to or contrasted with any other variety. There is only *one* ecology, and man is simply one element of it, and at present, a terribly destructive element at that. On every hand we are being warned that unless industrial society, and that includes all forms in the entire political spectrum, is almost instantly reformed, in only a few more years the world will be uninhabitable. It remains to be seen whether or not it is too late, particularly in view of the fact that so much of what we have done is irreversible. The following few chapters will present a more detailed study of some of the environmental destruction, produced by a burgeoning population, and the runaway industrial enterprise created to meet and profit from its unlimited material wants.

3

DEADLIER BY THE DOZEN

With the appearance of such books as Paul Ehrlich's *The Population Bomb,* Robert and Leona T. Rienow's *Moment in the Sun,* and William and Paul Paddock's *Famine—1975!,* and the recent upsurge of environmental concern, there cannot be many who are not familiar with the growing problem of population, even though many do not regard it as a serious one. There are many dimensions to the problem—food production, flourishing technology and its often disastrous by-products, housing, and simply the absolute limitation of sheer space.

We in the United States particularly need to face the population problem squarely. We have done precious little to alleviate it either in our own country or throughout the rest of the world. As a matter of fact, shipping surplus foods to undeveloped countries with runaway population growths would seem to encourage that growth while, at the same time, discouraging those countries from improving their agriculture while dreaming of becoming industrial states. Because our industrialized farming permits us to produce wheat more cheaply than many other nations in the hungry world, we additionally discourage potential indigenous agricultural production by the low prices on our exports.

Although there are hungry people in our country, some even starving, this is not the result of a shortage of food. And although we import a number of minerals vital to our industry, a situation which will worsen, our economy will for some time exhibit signs of growth. At the same time, the underdeveloped and undeveloped nations of the world are going to fall farther and farther behind. The United States is now using more than one half of all raw materials consumed each year by the entire world. As our wealth continues to exhibit itself, and the undeveloped nations fall farther behind as we use up their natural resources to appease consumer demand, we cannot long escape being cast as the "blue meanies" of the world. A great portion of the citizenry of the United States, in their pride and arrogance, are unaware that our involvement in Southeast Asia has altered world opinion, and we have replaced Russia as the world's imperialistic menace. When the people of the world, in increasing deprivation, come to realize that one fifteenth of the world population requires more raw materials than the balance of the combined nations, our affluence will cease to be a goal to emulate and will become the object of bitter resentment. As underdeveloped nations increase in population, we will cease to be even one fifteenth of the world's population, without at the same time ceasing to need the import of increasing amounts of raw materials.

As worldwide communication continues to grow, there will soon be few people who are not aware of the vast disparity in living standards between the population of the 25 percent of the rich nations and the 75 percent comprising the poor nations. It is not necessary to be literate to gain this message from a transistor radio, and someone has estimated, for example, that in Latin America alone it would be difficult to uncover any twenty-mile stretch of road which would not yield at least one transistor radio. We in this country must come to understand the dimensions of worldwide population crisis, both from our own point of view and from that of the world. While probing the dimensions of the problem itself, we must look at possible (and impossible) solutions. There is not much time left before the population explosion will force itself upon the consciousness of the entire world, either through famine, pestilence, or worldwide violence.

It is difficult not to drown in a sea of statistics when speaking of population growth, and impossible to discuss it without their use. Most of them are grim. At the present population growth rate, hundreds of millions of people are going to starve in the relatively near future, regardless of any food program for production on which we embark. Worldwide population is at the present time doubling roughly at the rate of every thirty-seven years. The population of countries such as Egypt, India, and Israel and the nations of Latin America are doubling much more rapidly, some in only fifteen years. By the year 2000, with the present growth rate, world population will be approximately seven billion, and less than thirty-seven years later, say around 2028, it will be fourteen billion, fourteen times the number of people many ecologists believe to be the optimum number for the world to sustain at a decent level of living. Food production would need to be twenty-five times the present level, and practically all the productive arable land is now in use. Just in order to feed adequately the present world population of three and one half billion, food production now would have to be doubled.

Technology, whether in the arena of space travel or increased food production, is certainly no answer. Space is obviously hostile to man, and instead of offering a limitless frontier, actually is itself a limitation. Supposing, however, that exporting excess population were feasible, and we had someplace to export it, in order to maintain a stable population of the present level, we would have to export eight thousand people per hour beginning now and continuing from now on at present growth rates. Garrett Hardin, of the University of California at Santa Barbara, has calculated that at the present cost of space travel, and using extremely optimistic assumptions, not the least of which is actually producing the necessary equipment, Americans, by cutting their standard of living by 82 percent could in one year save sufficient money to finance the exportation to the stars of one day's increase in population.[27] For those who believe that the earth could adequately sustain ten billion people, a population projection for the year 2025, stabilization at that level would require the exportation of excess people at a rate of twenty-five thousand per hour. Rush hour in space, anyone?

At the present rate of growth, in a little more than three hundred years, the total land area of the world will become a single city.[28] In a few thousand years, everything in the visible universe would be converted into solid people, and the ball of people would be expanding at the speed of light.[29] Not only will space travel not solve the problem, we must not be lulled into the complacent thought that "miracle" farming of both land and water can solve the problem—it is simply not so, and this particular aspect of the so-called solution will be dealt with in greater detail in the next chapter.

Doubling present population will create the necessity of increasing by more than double *all* commodities, including food production (ten thousand people are dying of starvation daily at the present level of production). Housing, clothing, furniture, appliances, highways, schools, hospitals, even in the prosperous United States, are already too few and too crowded. When we are unable to provide even subsistence level of food for our present population, how can we possibly hope to do anything but ensure mass disaster with an increasing population?

Not many of the developed countries of the world, whose populations are growing at the rate of doubling within fifty to one hundred years, can currently adequately feed their present populations, and none actually does. There are only ten countries in the world which produced more food in 1966 than they consumed: the United States, Canada, Australia, Argentina, France, New Zealand, Burma, Thailand, Rumania, and South Africa.[30] The United States produced about one half the surplus; Canada and Australia, most of the balance. All other countries found it necessary to import more food than they exported. In the "developing" countries of the world, such as in Latin America, Asia, and Africa, the number of people is increasing three times faster than the production of food to feed them. What is a problem of the quality of life in the developed countries is a problem of life itself in the undeveloped countries. There is less food per capita throughout the world today than there was during the depression, thirty years ago.

One of the most terrifying aspects of the situation in the rapidly growing countries is the age level of the present population. For example, in Costa Rica, which is doubling every seventeen years, chiefly because of the lowering of the death rate, 50 percent of the population is under the age of fifteen. The approach of these young people to their reproductive years is the reason for the dire predictions concerning the population explosion.[31] Unless the death rate and the birth rate pace each other, the rate of population growth will not change. Currently, Costa Rica has a birth rate of forty-one per 1,000, and a death rate of nine per 1,000. True, everyone must die sometime, but meanwhile the number of people in the world grows at an increasing rate, and it has been a half century since there has been an epidemic of major proportions resulting in a significant number of deaths. In 1919, twenty-five million people died of influenza.[32] Birth rates remain fairly stable. The increasing population is a result of the lowering death rate, which continues to decline. The world death rate fell from twenty-five per 1,000 in 1935 to sixteen per 1,000 in 1965, with a 1980 projection of twelve and seven tenths per 1,000. The worldwide rates are not so dramatic as the rates in nonindustrial, undeveloped countries.[33] The dramatic drop is not altogether a result of medical expertise; it is partly because populations have a higher percentage of young people. In Latin America, for example, by 1975 there will be 60 percent more marriages than in 1960—this is a result of population already *here*. No new drives for birth control will eliminate those already born.

During the year 1966, a year in which the population increased by seventy million, food production did not increase at all. The Paddocks in their book, *Famine— 1975!*, state that we had then turned a last corner on population and food production. Since that time there has been the so-called Green Revolution (discussed in more detail in the following chapter) and in 1969 the harvest of wheat was the greatest the world has ever known. This was the happy result of fortuitously good weather, completely undependable, and new strains of grain, not altogether satisfactory and acceptable. Even with bumper harvests, India and Pakistan are requesting seven million tons of food this year, and India's population is growing at the rate of one million people per month. She expects to have two hundred million more people by the year 1980, an increase equivalent to the entire present population of the United States on a land area roughly 42 percent of the contiguous states.

India's problem of overpopulation has been officially recognized by the government since 1951, but it has been monumentally unsuccessful in curtailing population growth effectively. Compulsory sterilization of men with more than three children has been advanced by some. A revelation of the immensity of the problem is the realization that even if those qualifying were actually to be found, it would take one thousand surgeons operating eight hours per day, five days a week, a full eight years to sterilize current candidates.[34] During the years of active campaigning by the Indian government, the population growth rate rose from 1.3 percent to 3 percent per year. In a 1969 study of India's population growth, Emerson Foote discovered that after seventeen years of family planning, only 6 to 7 percent of childbearing couples use any form of contraceptive, and the population has been growing more rapidly than before any birth-control programs. At the current rate of growth, India can expect to have one billion people by the year 2000.[35] Clearly, we cannot expect world population to come under control, either by depending on education or on the responsible reduction of growth by the rest of the world. Nor can we preach population control to the rest of the world without ourselves becoming responsible.

Actually, concentrating on countries like India does not really get to the heart of the problem. Wayne H. Davis, in an article in the *New Republic* entitled "Overpopulated America," states that we should refer to American population in terms of "Indian Equivalents," and says a conservative Indian Equivalent for one average American citizen is about twenty-five Indians.[36] He goes on to say that our per capita gross national product is thirty-eight times that of India, and much of our goods and services contribute to the decline of the ability of the environment to support life and the permanent depletion of the world's resources. India is a convenient target, when speaking of population growth, but we must not forget that portions of Africa and most of Latin America are equally in trouble. Most of these areas rely heavily on food importation, and it has already been noted that only a mere ten countries in the world produced more food than they consumed. It must be apparent that mass starvation is the logical outcome when people production surpasses food production throughout the world.

Garrett Hardin, in "The Tragedy of the Commons," [37] speaks of "no technical solution problems," and so classifies the population problem. Exponential growth of population necessarily means that the per capita share of the world's resources will decrease. Maximizing population does not, unfortunately, maximize goods. Whether or not Adam Smith and his followers intended to assert that individual decisions concerning one's own gain invariably result in promoting the public interest (*laissez faire*), that spirit remains from his work. The principle of *laissez faire,* when applied to reproduction, presents us with the problem of reexamining our freedom to reproduce as we choose.

Hardin relates population growth to the commons, i.e., that property which is held in common by all men in a given community. Considering a pasture held in common, it would be expected that each herdsman would try to keep as many cattle as possible on the commons, since each man is concerned with his own gain. That would perhaps work for many years, while population is controlled through war and disease, and cattle through poaching. At the time that social stability becomes a reality, a new dimension enters the picture. Population being freed from debilitating factors will grow rapidly, producing more herdsmen and necessarily more cattle. Secondly, the cattle of the herdsmen, freed from poaching by the stable society, will likewise increase. Finally, it will continue to be apparent, even in the face of overgrazing, that each herdsman's self-interest is best served by putting as many cattle on the commons as is possible for him, since each herdsman gains individually from the sale of his own cattle. But it must be apparent also that each herdsman shares in the problem of overgrazing. That, says Hardin, is the tragedy—"Each man is locked into a system that compels him to increase his herd without limit—in a world that is limited. . . . Freedom in a commons brings ruin to all." [38] Both land and sea suffer from survival of the philosophy of the commons, which in this instance becomes the entire earth. The freedom to breed, when coupled with the idea that everyone has an equal right to the commons can lead to nothing but tragedy. Each man feels free to reproduce at will expecting the produce from the commons to feed and clothe him and his. The Universal Declaration of Human Rights espoused by the United Nations expressly states the right of each man to determine the size of his family.

Each man also expects that the commons will survive whatever wastes he dumps into it. The pollution problem is one of population. While an old adage about running water being able to purify itself every ten miles might have been close enough to the truth with only one family dumping waste into it, a family every one hundred feet along the same ten-mile stretch doing the same would render the adage false and result in tragedy for the stream. When all streams are being fouled, the problem of property rights becomes one which must be carefully rethought.

As population increases, the commons must be replaced by "private" property in the interests of self-preservation, but how is the world to be fenced to ensure self-preservation? Who can "fence" the air? Establishment of a three-mile, twelve-mile, or even a hundred-mile sea limit will not fence the marine life therein—or the chemical or radioactive wastes dumped by any nation.

What technical solution can rescue the world from the misery of overpopulation? The pill? IUD? None of the contraceptives now known and available has proved efficacious in solving the problem. Hegel has stated, "Freedom is the recognition of necessity." Only man's recognition of the necessity of limiting the freedom to breed, and a worldwide society organized to enforce that limitation by denying access to the life-sustaining products of the "commons," can save the world from ultimate ruin.

The *scientific* answer to solving the problem of feeding the world's burgeoning population is that there is *no* scientific answer. Our crude technology (crude compared to the results of nature's two billion years of experimentation) cannot be allowed further to devastate our limited landscape, searching for hit-or-miss solutions. The solution is self-evident—halt the population growth and slowly begin to decrease our numbers, responsibly accepting a world

populated with older and older people, and fewer and
fewer young people, delightful as they are, until our agriculture can support the existing people without technological coercion. Only accidentally has technology proved
corrective—in the state of Madras in India, where 80 percent of the villages have electricity, the number of births is
less than one half the national average! [39]

We in the United States have scarcely more than begun
to recognize that there is a problem, here or elsewhere,
and our merchandising philosophy has created and continues to create a climate most inconducive to responsible
education and action. Everything has been endowed with
sexual appeal by Madison Avenue and women's maga-
zines—to say nothing of *Playboy*. Industry gloats over the
ever-increasing production of additional customers, without the accompanying sober thought that each new baby
may be potentially among the unemployed, a consumer of
sorts, but a sorry and unhappy one. Everything from
deodorants to detergents is hawked through sexual appeal.
Neither the government nor our schools have begun a responsible education program to address the problem.
While our erotically-oriented advertising can be discounted by well-educated, rational, responsible people, we
are doing nothing to educate or curtail the unthinking,
irrational procreation of those who are poorly educated or
incapable of conducting their lives in a responsible manner. We, as a nation, are, consciously or not, encouraging
the propagation of those least able to plan and care for the
future of the nation. Irresponsible neglect of the future of
our children should not be excused in the name of free
enterprise. If we continue to refuse to engage in extensive
and accountable educational practices in the field of sex,
as well as some form of population control, we are auto-

matically dedicating the future of our nation and our children to what has been termed as "frontal-lobe deficients" by Dr. William Shockley, Nobel Prize physicist.[40]

No matter what religious myths we regard as "holy," wanton human suicide by fecundity and subsequent overpopulation can scarcely be pleasing to God, rather the epitome of a sinful disregard of the charge to be faithful stewards of this beautiful vineyard we call the earth. The result in this country is that something like one in four children lives in poverty—surely there is no excuse for this. According to Sylvia Porter, the economist, almost one half of the children in the United States in families with five or more children live in poverty—five times the rate of those in families with one child.[41] We must not be distracted by cries of "genocide" from the poor, the black, the brown. It is not only the poor and the minority groups which are involved, it is the entire nation. Neither cries of "genocide" nor excuses of "wealth" can be used as pious excuses for producing too many offspring, for destruction of our land and resources will not respect either color or wealth. When our agricultural land is destroyed by overuse and misuse, even the wealthy will find it difficult to import food in a world where only ten nations export food. When our air is contaminated from overproduction of power and automobiles, wealth cannot buy fresh, pure air, and charity cannot provide it for the poor. Nor can wealth purchase potable water when our water resources are irretrievably fouled. All of our problems of pollution are inseparably linked to problems of overpopulation.

Of the one hundred ninty thousand people being added to world population every day, more than one half will lead lives dominated by hunger and privation. Although the growth of the United States population is a small percentage of this, we are doing less to implement population decrease than Egypt or China. Although slow to start, and then only motivated by free money for the purpose, Egypt now has a massive educational campaign, augmented by governmental action. There are some two thousand birth-control centers which provide information, intrauterine loops, or the pill for a few cents per month.[42] China, likewise, has recognized the extent of her problems, and to encourage smaller families, gives extra clothing rations to those who do not marry until they are over thirty; those who have more than three children are denied cotton coupons for more children, and, according to current information, food for more than three children is now being curtailed. This news from China is particularly encouraging, since their present approach appears to be one aimed at curtailment rather than simply education. Education often is too late to help solve the problem. For example, in the early years of the Hong Kong Family Planning Association, the women who sought assistance were typically over the age of thirty and already had an average of six children.[43] This situation prevails throughout much of the undeveloped world where four or five children are considered the ideal number.

What have we done and what are we doing to curtail our own population growth? Criminally little. Yet, we, as a burgeoning nation, are far more responsible for the environmental crisis than countries such as India with more than double our population. Annually, we are spending roughly the same amount of money on rat control as on population control, and most of what we are spending goes into what is commonly referred to as "family planning." If a family *plans* to have five children, it is still at least three too many. Large families tend to generate large families, and yet the horror attendant upon the results of some simple arithmetic should make every young married couple seriously consider limiting the size of their family. As Dr. Ehrlich points out, if the descendants of a family with ten children each had ten children, by the tenth generation they would have peopled the earth with ten billion people, or roughly three times the entire world population today.[44]

At the present level of the crisis, there appears to be no avenue open to legislators other than economic sanctions, an avenue already pursued in China. Senator Robert Packwood of Oregon has offered a bill to the Senate which would financially penalize those who have more than two children. This is, of course, discriminatory, and would allow, while nonetheless penalizing, the wealthy to produce progeny as desired, while discouraging procreation among the poor. In this sense, the bill is very unfair, but neither the wealthy nor the poor comprise the bulk of our population, nor account for the major portion of our growth, which comes from the great middle portion of our people. With the cost of education and the increasing desire to provide it for our children, economic sanctions would undoubtedly make someone with a middle income thoughtful about producing more than one or two children. Certainly, until disaster is imminent, worse yet, perhaps even actual, this is the only avenue open. At present, it being difficult even to obtain sterilization voluntarily, there is no likelihood of an arbitrary imposition of it on those who have more than two children, and "1984" style of proposals concerning birth control through our water supplies, or some other such means, are not only clearly unacceptable philosophically and theologically, but they are not feasible technologically without known disastrous side effects, not to mention unforeseen consequences.

The necessity to curtail population growth is upon us,

and we as the richest nation in the world must assume world leadership in this area. We could assure the world of our concern and seriousness by using the pressure of economic sanctions to limit population growth, and at the same time relieve the pressure of producing children among the poor to provide "extra hands" by an intelligent system of income support and assured economic security for the elderly and the handicapped. Then the people who have the children which create the need for increased services—schools, housing, water, trash disposal, hospital care—would be the people paying for them. If having large families makes life meaningful to some couples, they would simply have to take their pleasures from the children themselves, without the added pleasure of affluence at the expense of society as a whole. If original economic sanctions do not bring about zero population growth (and Senator Packwood's bill would be only a mild antidote), then economic penalties could be increased until stabilization has become a reality.

Aside from assuming leadership in the field of enlightened education and providing readily available contraceptives for our population, as well as imposing economic sanctions on those families with more than two children, as a nation we need to engage in a basic reevaluation of our foreign-aid policy. The Paddocks, in their book, *Famine—1975!*, have suggested that we, like medical centers in time of war, divide our "patients" into three categories—those who will die no matter what you do, those who will live no matter what you do, and those who need immediate help in order to survive. Should not our aid be concentrated on the latter nations, with the clear-cut understanding that such aid would not be forthcoming if the nation showed signs of using it as a crutch for population and agricultural business as usual? They suggest that this might mean that Libya would probably not need aid, since, with their vast oil resources, they can import necessary food, whereas West Pakistan, which shows signs of responsible leadership and action, would be greatly helped by aid. On the other hand, India appears to be one of those patients who have reached such a disparity between population growth and food production that any aid we send is simply prolonging the agony of its demise. Heartless? Is it desirable to spread our aid over the whole world, equally, with the result that no one's problems are resolved and the level of misery for all gradually increases? No rational physician would put a patient with a severe communicable disease in a room with someone in the hospital simply for a checkup just to be democratically fair. Aid which is now going to India could be diverted to a patient that appears still to be on the "hope" list. Such action, of course, could by no means replace education and action on the home front.

Much is made of "freedom of choice" for deciding the size of private, individual families, without a concomitant discussion of the lack of freedom in hunger and deprivation, to say nothing of the loss of human dignity in overpopulated countries. At the present time, this is the basic situation in undeveloped countries chiefly, but without change it will soon become a lack of freedom throughout the world. Many of our rights are being eroded by overpopulation—the right to privacy, the right to live in a clean environment unthreatened by polluted air and water and poisonous pesticides, the right to silence, open space, and wilderness.

The effects of overcrowding among animals is well known to experimental psychologists—extreme overcrowding among rats in one study resulted in cannibalism and sexual deviation among the males, and in increased miscarriages, a lack of interest in their young, and indifference to nest-building among the females. The effects of overcrowding on humans are also evident. In countries now disastrously overcrowded, human indifference to human misery is shocking. In Japan, help is rarely extended to a person who drops, perhaps dying, on a crowded street. In India, the starving beggar is scarcely noticed in passing. In China, the individual is not even recognized as important.

Perhaps the worst situation is in Latin America. In a report in *The Population Council*, Dr. Alfredo Aguirre states that in a rural village of Colombia people are multiplying so rapidly that the entire community has broken down.[45] Large families are crowded into shacks, there is not enough food, and what there is goes to the fathers who must work in the fields. Children starve or suffer the results of malnutrition—mental and physical retardation. Adolescents become educational dropouts and socially alienated. The homicide rate is the highest in the world and family life is unstable. There is a high birthrate of illegitimate children, with an accompanying rise in child abandonment and "masked infanticide," where small children are allowed to die of starvation or from disease without seeking medical aid. Requests for death certificates for children are made with no apparent anguish or emotion.

Is Calcutta to be the city of the future? There six hundred thousand people sleep, eat, and live in the streets, "ragged skeletons, barefoot, hollow-eyed, blinking their apathetic stares out of grey dusty faces." [46] The starving people from the countryside crowd into the city seeking help, and wait in endless lines for a handout of Midwestern grain. Mass starvation has not and does not in any imminent future threaten the Western world, with the exception of Latin America, but many of the other problems of overcrowding do. We are already suffering from lack of adequate housing, urban crowding, nightmarish traffic, diminished and faulty public service, increasing water shortages, air, water, and soil pollution, overcrowded hospitals and schools, rising crime rates, and everywhere noise, noise, noise! Soon, clearly soon, man is going to have to learn to accommodate his fecundity to the ability of the earth to sustain him.

4

FARMING OUR WAY TO FAMINE

There have been those, concerned with various problems of pollution, particularly water pollution, who have declared, in all seriousness, that environmental demise was firmly assured with the invention of the flush toilet. As facetious as that appears, there is a great deal of truth in the statement, at least so far as water pollution is concerned, not simply because of modern plumbing, but because man is the only land-based mammal who deposits his wastes in water, and expects rivers, streams, lakes, and the seas to dispose of them. In truth, nature, as always wiser than the combined wisdom of men, has provided the perfect "filter" and purifier for wastes, and that is the soil. Nature's wastes are deposited back onto the soil, where they provide natural enrichment necessary for the soil to produce plants. Those wastes which would "injure" bodies of water are efficiently filtered and purified by the soil. Very few municipalities recycle their water back to the land, although research has proved this to be practical in a number of ways. Pennsylvania State University and the neighboring town of State College have been experimenting since 1963 with such a system.[47] Previously, their effluents had been given secondary treatment and dumped into a river which eventually ran into Spring Creek, with predictable results. Spring Creek became filled with algae, and the desirable trout were being replaced by suckers. The oxygen level had been changed by the increase of nitrates and phosphates introduced into the water.

Not only the water in the creek was affected, but millions of gallons of water were being pumped from the underground water supply, treated, pumped as waste into the creek and carried out to sea, instead of being channeled back to the land and eventually back to the underground supply. The ground water was being depleted more rapidly than it could be replaced by rain.

The experiment over the ensuing years has proved very successful. The sewage has solids removed and the water is carried by pipe and sprinkled on agricultural and forest lands. The water seeps through the soil and is eventually returned to the water table. The nutrients in the water, nitrates and phosphates, are recycled through trees and crops, in place of chemical fertilizers. The soil purifies the water and when it is once again pumped from wells, it is potable. Once again, it is sent from the sewage plant back to the soil, and the cycle is repeated. Although some trees were not favorably affected, by and large, favorable growth resulted in most and the water was saved at its source.

Obviously, the system works best near growing crops, but it would take only about 129 acres of land to dispose of one million gallons of waste water per day, and the productivity of the agricultural and forest land are improved in the process. Naturally, problems would vary from place to place, and it is more readily adaptable to small communities. Instead of centralized treatment plants in major communities, it would be possible to decentralize and have treatment plants at various diverse locations in the community. Certainly the system is far more sensible than dumping our waste products into the nearest stream or lake, even with the most sophisticated treatment.

The earth has suffered much under the improving hand of man. His inexorable tie to land, water, and air is not generally recognized by most people. Americans are largely urban creatures, living in a paved and plastic environment, and scarcely aware of the fact that city and industry are inescapably linked to the complexity of the biology of water and soil. City people do not spend many hours of their days pondering the fact that the continued existence of man depends on approximately nine inches of topsoil.

The impending crisis in the environment was not, as has been suggested, triggered by the invention of the flush toilet, devastating though modern sewage treatment has proved to be. It was the development of stable agricultural communities which has created so many of our environmental problems. It has been agricultural practices more than most of man's other activities, which has disturbed the ecological balance of nature. In order to feed increasing population, agricultural man cut back forests, removed cover from the soil, overfarmed and overgrazed the land and allowed the precious topsoil to wash away, never to be recovered. He has, with his machines, become increasingly efficient at cutting down forests, mining the soil, and exploiting water resources. All other physical needs of mankind remain secondary to food, short of emergencies when man's immediate physical safety is endangered by accident or disaster.

As the continents became populated, the natural balance of the soil cycle was disturbed by agricultural practices. More plants were grown than the soil was able to sustain, and as a result, the organic nutrients necessary for growing healthy crops were depleted more each year. Primitive agriculture, in sparsely populated areas, survived without undue soil damage simply because the cultivators periodically moved from one area to another. This allowed abandoned land to lie fallow and recover fertility on its own. On the other hand, areas such as the Fertile Crescent became almost total deserts as a result of overfarming and overgrazing. It is difficult for modern man to "remember" that parts of the Sahara were once some of the most fertile lands on earth.

When agricultural man discovered and moved to the "new world," westward migration to available virgin soils was always possible. As the continent was settled, crop production on all tillable soil was intensified to feed a growing population, depleting more and more soil nutrients. According to Barry Commoner, biologist at Washington University in St. Louis, the organic content of the soil in the Midwest has declined by 50 percent in the last one hundred years. The result has been declining harvests, unless man added either natural or artificial nutrients.[48]

As long as farmers used natural fertilizer, either plant or animal, organic nutrients were returned to the soil, but with the rapid growth of population and the end of the frontier, man began to use chemical inorganic fertilizer. Worse yet, he began to farm marginal lands. One of the more dramatic warnings from nature of the ultimate outcome to be expected from such farming was the "dust bowl" phenomenon of the 1930's in the Kansas, Oklahoma, and Texas wheat belts. The sky was frequently darkened at midday, not by clouds of moisture, but by rolling banks of choking, drifting, powder-fine dust. As it rolled through a town, man and beast fled in terror, and those who remained found it possible to breathe only through a wet towel. Sometimes it rained mud, sometimes only dust, but always it meant that man had transgressed the limits imposed by nature. In the United States, with the rapid growth of "scientific" farming and a developing chemical industry, a technological answer was sought to the need for ever-increasing yields.

In countries lacking our technological "blessings," where man has found it necessary to farm or graze on marginal lands, per acre yields continue to decline. For example, according to the Department of Agriculture, the corn yields per acre in Colombia, Venezuela, and Ecuador were higher from 1955 to 1959 than from 1961 to 1963. In Brazil, wheat and corn yields were higher from 1935 to 1939 than from 1955 to 1960. In Guatemala, the yields have fallen from 15.7 bushels per acre in 1939 to less than twelve in 1962.[49] Part of this drop resulted from putting into production land which was agriculturally marginal, a situation that is becoming increasingly necessary as population increases throughout the world.

With the growth of the chemical industry, it became possible to produce more convenient and cheaper inorganic fertilizers than natural plant or animal fertilizer. Even where the soil had been significantly depleted, fantastic growth in crop yields was possible. The magic potion seemed to have been discovered. Since World War II the use of inorganic nitrogen-based fertilizer has increased seven times. Massive chemical fertilizing practices have introduced increasing quantities of nitrogen, phosphorus, potassium, and other plant nutrients into the soil. Unfortunately, this is not an unmixed blessing. Chemical fertilizer tends to decrease the natural bacterial content of the soil, as well as discourage the earthworm population. Substitution of chemical fertilizer for natural fertilizer reduces soil humus, making the soil less friable. As a result, chemical fertilizers do not continue to work as effectively as at the outset of their use, and increased use of them becomes necessary. Chemical fertilizers do not build up topsoil as nature is capable of doing when left to her own devices. Besides making the soil addicted to these additives, the use of inorganic fertilizers is not without other serious and far-reaching environmental consequences.

Books dealing with almost any aspect of the environmental crisis tend to become statistical nightmares. Perhaps a simple way of examining the complex problem of the interrelationship of soil, water, and nutrients is to study in depth one specific agricultural area. Data is readily available for the San Joaquin Valley in California because a great deal of study has been done there. The Valley is additionally interesting because, while extremely fertile, it can be in a sense considered marginal, since it could not be farmed as extensively as it is today without irrigation. Approaching a study of agricultural practices in this Valley introduces several interlocking phenomena, not the least of which is that soil and water (domestic, industrial, or agricultural) are inseparable partners.

The central valley of California consists of varied terrain with very different amounts of rainfall and water available for agricultural purposes. The San Joaquin Valley is about 40 miles wide and roughly 450 miles long in a north-south direction. It is closed on the north and south, and surrounded by a mountain wall broken in only a single place—a gap behind the Golden Gate Bridge at San Francisco. Through this single gap passes the entire drainage of the Valley. It encompasses an area comprised of about

18,000 square miles. There are two major rivers, the Sacramento and the San Joaquin, which drain the interior basin. Four major mountain streams flow into the Valley from the western slope of the Sierra Nevada, and eight major streams flow into the Valley from the south, making some 8,000,000 fertile acres among the best agricultural land in the country.

In addition to the natural water contained in the rivers and streams, beneath the Valley floor are deep water-bearing formations composed in an earlier geologic age, which have a water storage capacity far greater than all surface reservoirs, now built or proposed. This latter supply of natural water is superior to water stored in surface reservoirs, in that it takes up no land space, is not depleted by evaporation, and being everywhere present, need not be transported and distributed. With the introduction of surface irrigation and chemical fertilizer, however, the presence of this vast amount of underground water has created grave problems. Before the introduction of sophisticated and complex irrigation practices, agriculture in the Valley depended on the water from natural streams and rivers, plus the underground water. These, however, have proved either insufficient, undependable, or too expensive to use in extensive agriculture.

With exploding population, water for irrigation and for industrial and urban use has become an increasing problem.[50] More than 80 percent of the annual precipitation occurs during the five months of winter and spring, and is so unreliable that it varies as much as 50 percent from dry to wet years. Irrigation was introduced into the Valley around 1780. After a slow beginning, it grew rapidly, and by the end of the nineteenth century there were a million acres under irrigation.

The original irrigation water for the Valley was taken directly from the streams in the Valley floor. This water was supplemented during the dry season by pumped water from the underground reservoirs. By the end of the nineteenth century, the construction of dams and canals began to carry water from greater and greater distances. Early in the twentieth century, the natural water became insufficient to sustain the level of agriculture then in existence in the Valley. It became necessary to increase the amount of water available, and in the 1940's, the engineers made a major assault on the water system in the Valley. Two large dams were constructed, the Shasta on the Sacramento and the Friant on the San Joaquin. Two canals were constructed, the Friant-Kern and the Madera to carry water from the Friant Reservoir south and north along the east side of the Valley. The Delta Mendota Canal was constructed to carry water along the west side of the Valley to replace water taken from the San Joaquin River. As a result, the San Joaquin River's flow was diminished while it still served as a source of water as well as the principal drain for the Valley. Since 1945, the water remaining in the San Joaquin tributaries has been channeled into new canals (the California Aqueduct and the Eastside Canal). With the completion of the California Water Plan, the San Joaquin River becomes, in effect, not a river, but a mere drain, with, however, insufficient flow to function efficiently as such, and with water so polluted that it is useless even for agricultural purposes. Increasing the supply of agricultural water for use in the Valley, and at the same time crippling its only drainage system, has turned into an engineering nightmare.

The purpose of irrigation is to keep the top layers of soil constantly moist. As the water evaporates, it leaves behind minerals in the soil, making it necessary to flush these away with additional water, forcing the mineral-laden water down through the soil to the ground water. In order to alleviate the problem, the California Department of Water Resources and the Federal Bureau of Reclamation proposed construction of the San Luis Drain, which would discharge waters heavily laden with salt and chemicals into the eastern end of San Francisco Bay. The proposed drain would run 280 miles north from Bakersfield. It would be the only drain to carry excess agricultural water away from land newly irrigated by the California Aqueduct. Most of the four hundred thousand acres of the San Joaquin River delta, the entire San Joaquin and Sacramento Rivers below Hood, California, and the Sacramento ship channel to Sacramento itself will be affected. This drain plan was chosen over alternatives on the basis of cost. Behind the "necessity" for such a drain lies an intricate problem of salt balance in the soil.

The water carried in irrigation projects is certainly necessary in the Valley if it is to be tilled at the present level. This water, however, carries with it dissolved salts from its flow down the mountainsides. For example, the Colorado River carries into the Imperial Valley 1.25 tons of salt for every acre foot. Unalleviated accumulation of salt in the soil would, of course, quickly turn the San Joaquin Valley into the San Joaquin Desert, a process that has ominous historical precedents such as the Sahara Desert. It is estimated that 400 million tons of salt have built up in the San Joaquin Valley soil already, and in some places ground water contains sufficient salt to make it toxic for plant life. In order to counteract the problem, it has been necessary to introduce drainage tiles into farmlands to carry salt-laden water from the fields. Space between the drainage tiles in the Valley has diminished in the past twenty-five years from 300 feet to 50 feet in some places.[51] The purpose of the San Luis Drain is to carry these salt-laden waters to San Francisco Bay.

During the flight of Apollo 9, a picture was taken with infrared film 150 miles above California, Arizona, and New Mexico. Infrared film records green crops as red, and withered crops as green. In the picture the sharp color contrast at the international border between the United States and Mexico testifies to the necessity for removing excess salts from the soil. North of the border the fields appear as a deep red, and south of the border, where Mexican farmers cannot afford the expense of drainage tiles, the picture, belying actuality, is a bright green.[52]

The practice of irrigation, plus the seepage of water from irrigation canals, results in a fluctuating water table. As this water percolates up and down through the soil it dissolves more and more of the salts, finally becoming so laden that its presence is toxic to plant life. Nowhere is the destructive evidence of irrigation practices more compelling than in Egypt in connection with the Aswân Dam. In the first instance, it has deprived the flood plains of annual fertilization, making the use of chemical fertilizers a necessity for decent harvests, wiped out the sardine fishing industry because the fish were deprived of flood-carried nutrients which resulted in an alarming incidence of schistosomiasis, a debilitating disease of the liver, in approximately 70 percent of the population in the vicinity of the water. This disease organism depends on snails, which depend on a steady supply of water, such as provided by controlled irrigation. But further, practice of controlled irrigation below the dam is resulting in salination of the soil, and unless measures are introduced to control the process, the irrigated land will become a desert.

It may seem harmless to drain the salt-laden waters into

San Francisco Bay, when after all, the San Joaquin River has always drained water from the Valley into the Bay. But drainage water from the Valley will not contain merely the usual natural mixture of the salts of the ocean, and there are potentially fatal hazards ahead for the Bay if the San Luis Drain is finally completed. The salts it will carry are significantly dangerous because they contain large quantities of chemical radicals of nitrogen, phosphorus, potassium, calcium, magnesium, and sulfur, which serve as nutrients to plants and phytoplankton. These chemicals are readily leached from the heavily fertilized soil by rains and irrigation. These nutrients in the water increase the algae growing there, which in turn decrease the amount of oxygen. This process will speed up eutrophication and eventually result in a dead body of water, such as Lake Erie. This is the future prospect for San Francisco Bay with the waste water from the San Joaquin Valley being drained into it.

Because of drainage problems, not only are the rivers, lakes, and the San Francisco Bay endangered, but water in communal and domestic wells is threatened. A number of communal wells have had to be closed in California because nitrates have been leached from the soil and have contaminated the water in them. The problem, incidentally, is not confined to California. Over a three-year period, fourteen infant deaths were attributed to nitrate poisoning from well water in Minnesota,[53] and there are wells scattered through the Midwestern agricultural area similarly affected.

In December, 1966, the McFarland, California, water department included a warning with its bills that the municipal water supply was no longer considered safe for infant consumption.[54] There was fear that the presence of nitrates in the water might result in incidents of methemoglobinemia (infant cyanosis), which is a depletion of oxygen in the blood and is sometimes fatal. Two months later, the neighboring town of Delano issued a similar warning. Three of Delano's wells were found to contain nitrate levels 100 percent above that designated by the Federal Government as safe. At the present time, nitrate contamination threatens the water supply of a large portion of California.

In an extensive survey, carried out by the Bureau of Sanitary Engineering, it was discovered that nitrate contamination of wells followed a random pattern, leading to the conclusion that a large portion of ground water beneath extensive areas of California was involved. The water of Delano was subjected to a meticulous investigation by the Water Resources Board. Delano lies at the southern end of the San Joaquin Valley. It was May, 1967, before the investigation yielded answers. These were apparent in an agricultural report released by the Sierra Vista Ranch. This ranch is situated over an area where the water table had been drastically lowered during a long period of irrigation by pumping well water, and subsequently raised by seeping irrigation water carried by the Friant-Kern Canal.

When large amounts of water are drained through soil located in low rainfall areas, such as the Valley, the original nitrates are washed down through the soil with it, as well as additional nitrates applied in the form of fertilizer. When irrigation first began to be used in the Valley, water was pumped from underground and poured over the surface. It then percolated down through the soil carrying natural and artificial nitrates. Because of evaporation, only a small percentage of the water returned to the underground reservoirs, causing the water table to drop. This pattern continued in the Valley for one hundred years. Irrigation water was leaching nitrates from the surface, and at the same time the water table was dropping. The process hastened after World War I when irrigation became more intense and inorganic fertilizers came to be used increasingly. The water in the wells of the Sierra Vista Ranch dropped from 144 feet in 1927, to 304 feet below the surface in 1951. When the Friant-Kern Canal was completed in 1951, the pattern was altered with a drastic reduction in pumping. The water from the canal, however, continued leaching the nitrates from the soil, and with reduced pumping, plus the introduction of this water from the outside, the water table began to rise. As it did so, it carried up through the soil the nitrates which had accumulated during the previous one hundred years. Studies conducted in the early 1960's established the fact that there was a concentration of nitrates at about a twenty-foot level below the surface of the farmland which had been irrigated over a period of from eleven to fourteen years. Adjacent lands, which had not been irrigated, showed no such concentration. It could be expected that the lower the water table, the deeper the concentration of nitrates.

The farmland around Delano had been in use for a much longer period of time, and there the nitrate levels, following the above pattern, would be expected to be much deeper. Water rising through a deeper and more extensive concentration of soil contaminated with nitrates would become increasingly contaminated. It was demonstrated in the drinking water of Delano that nitrate levels are always higher when the water table is rising than they are when it is falling. Nitrate levels have been steadily rising in the Valley, as well as throughout the agricultural land in the entire country. The concentration of nitrates in the water to be carried into San Francisco Bay by the proposed San Luis Drain is predicted to be at least twice that designated as safe by the Federal Government. This water would be introduced to underground natural reservoirs when it leaves the drain and enters the San Joaquin River delta.

Having no technologically feasible solution to the problem of concentration of nitrates in underground water, California has, in effect, instituted a policy of not notifying the general public when nitrate levels are above standards, even as high as double the standards, preferring to believe, apparently, that what people don't know won't hurt them. Certain public officials are notified, but no course of public action is suggested or required of them. Since California uses more fertilizer than any other state (twice the next user), the situation can only get worse. In California, fertilizer may be applied at a rate as high as one thousand pounds of nitrate per acre. Even if large-scale draining were instituted, disposal of the effluence remains an unsolved problem. As noted above, the problem is not exclusive with California, and widespread, indiscriminate use of nitrogen fertilizers could pose a health hazard anywhere chemical fertilizing and irrigation are part of the agricultural practice.

The above picture of the San Joaquin Valley agriculture has not included mention of a problem with which even the unsophisticated are now familiar, and that is the use of pesticides in farming. Along with chemically fertilized farming, the industrial one-crop farm has resulted in the necessity for chemical pesticides, the ultimate effect of which is yet to be revealed in terms of their total ravage of our environment. The planting of vast sections of the

country with single crops—wheat, corn, cotton, tobacco—
has an easily predictable outcome; it provides a readily
accessible banquet for the particular enemies of that
crop.

Alarm among the ecologically informed has grown with
increasing uses of "hard" pesticides, such as DDT, aldrin,
dieldrin, and endrin. Synthetic pesticide production in the
United States was 124,259,000 pounds in 1947. It rose to
637,666,000 pounds in 1960 and is still soaring, with the
chemical industry having more and more at stake in their
sale and use. As agricultural pests have become resistant
and immune to their effects, farmers have more and more
come to depend upon the use of stronger, but shorter-lived
pesticides such as the organophosphates, which are highly
toxic to man. These shorter-lived pesticides must be applied at more frequent intervals than the residual pesticides. When any of the synthetic organic pesticides are
effective, they wipe out the major portion of the pest population, predators leave, and only resistant strains of pests
remain. They multiply rapidly without enemies to keep
them under control, and the resulting situation is worse
than before chemical pest control was instituted.

For example, the cotton industry of Peru collapsed in
1956, chiefly as a result of massive use of synthetic organic pesticides. In 1943, before introduction of the pesticides, the per acre yield of cotton in the Cañete Valley was
406 pounds. The first residual pesticides were used in
1949, and the per acre yield jumped to 649 pounds by
1954. However, by that time the list of crop pests had
grown from seven to thirteen and several had become
resistant to DDT and BHC. Within ten years the per acre
yield of cotton had dropped to 296 pounds, even though
the application of pesticides was more frequent and more

expensive. In the face of economic disaster, Peru forbade the use of the synthetic chemical pesticides, and the farmers returned to the use of mineral insecticides, such as lead or arsenic.[55] This experience in Peru is by no means unique.

The use of DDT and similar residual pesticides inevitably results in the growth of resistant strains of pests. In 1946, some populations of houseflies were reported as resistant to DDT. By 1948, the list of pest species showing resistance to the new organic insecticides had grown to 12. By 1957, there were 76 and they have been increasing steadily ever since. A total of 224 pest insects resistant to modern insecticides are now known. These include 97 insects of public health or veterinary importance, and 127 which attack field and forest crops and stored products.[56]

When stronger nonpersistent pesticides, such as the organophosphates, are substituted, they must be applied more frequently. Their toxicity kills practically all of the pests in a field, and because the pesticides are quickly broken down, pests from neighboring fields invade the sprayed area, which no longer contains natural enemies, and multiply rapidly. Entomologists at the University of California, in a study of the use of organophosphates, discovered that damage to cotton from bollworms in sprayed areas was higher than that in unsprayed areas.[57]

The organophosphates constitute a health menace. In one county in southern California, the health commissioner was conducting a routine health survey of young people and accidentally discovered that more than one half of them were suffering from organophosphate poisoning. They lived in a farming community and played or worked in the fields that had been sprayed with organophosphates. There are untold incidences of pesticide poisoning among farm workers, and man is only one of many living creatures affected. (Since that time, the Department of Agriculture has revealed that over the past several years there have been 123 deaths from organophosphate poisoning.) In a study of a 12¼-mile stretch of field which had been sprayed with one of the more lethal varieties, 365 dead birds were discovered. The surmise is that they died because they had eaten insects or berries in the sprayed area.[58]

Practically everyone is familiar, at least to some extent, with the devastating effects of the chlorinated hydrocarbons, such as DDT, on wildlife. Twenty-five years after the first widespread use of these hard pesticides, we have learned that even tiny amounts can drastically alter animal life. Birds of prey are diminishing rapidly, and many species will soon disappear entirely—the peregrine falcon, sparrow hawks, and the gold and the bald eagles are some on the critical list. When they disappear, the ecological balance will change because these birds are predators of rodents. Rapid increase in the rodent population is to be expected. The pesticide DDT reduces the bird population by interfering with the calcium metabolism, causing thin-shelled, nonviable eggs. During an experiment in which one group of ducks was fed DDE, the form of DDT they would ordinarily encounter in the environment, and one group of ducks was used as a control group, 24 percent of the eggs of the ducks which were fed the DDE cracked or broke, compared with only 4 percent of the eggs of the control group. Even when the eggs remained intact in the first group, only between one third and one half of the surviving ducklings were healthy.[59]

The pesticide problem is by no means confined to the North American continent, as is evident from the Peruvian cotton incident noted above. An Associated Press news release in a recent newspaper stated that two Soviet farmers had accidentally killed more than fifty cranes, two hundred rare great bustards, eleven gray geese, and fifty foxes by the careless use of chemical pesticides. This major catastrophe is only one incident resulting from a widening abuse of chemicals by Soviet agriculture. Conservationist Vladimir Peskov asks: "Why do we see almost no flocks of geese and cranes in April? . . . Almost all the partridges are gone. Our woods, gardens, and fields are becoming quieter and quieter." The duck-hunting season was canceled across the Soviet during 1969 because of the shortage of ducks.[60] Not only wildlife are victims. Pesticides rank fifth among harmful substances most frequently ingested by children. In the United States four thousand children under the age of five were poisoned by pesticides last year.

The hard pesticides have, in addition, become an atmospheric hazard. Monitored rainwater in Great Britain between August, 1966, and July, 1967, revealed residues of BHC, dieldrin, DDT, DDE, DDD, and some traces of heptachlor epoxide. One of the sampling stations was Lerwick, in the Shetland Islands, the station farthest removed from any agricultural activity. Levels there were equal in dieldrin and the DDT group, and higher in BHC than any other station. The Shetlands are surrounded by sea, and about the only pesticides used are for annual sheep-dipping. The British rainwater study indicated that pesticides are airborne throughout the year, and calculations based on that study reveal that hundreds, possibly thousands, of tons of pesticides are being rained on the Atlantic each year. The atmosphere is responsible for transporting larger quantities of pesticides throughout the world than any other mechanism involved. Heavy concentrations of pesticides enter the atmosphere during storms which pick up pesticide-laden dust, but most of them entering the atmosphere probably enter directly as vapors.[61] Levels of these pesticides increase the farther one moves up the food chain, and man is at the top of the food chain. No one knows how much buildup in the tissues of man and other animals is tolerable, or what will be the end result of that buildup.

Emphasizing the damage occurring in wildlife from the use of pesticides, however, is perhaps to miss completely an aspect of the problem which is basically more serious and that is the assumption behind their use that they are effective pest *controllers*. Kenneth E. F. Watt states that it is not a fact, it is an assumption, that pesticides actually *control* pests.[62] Experiments by agricultural entomologists in Southeast Asia following World War II on bagworm in oil palm plantations revealed that the highest concentrations of pests were where pesticides had been applied. Moving away from those sites the concentration of pests diminished. This is just another instance of the fallacy the chemical industry has perpetrated, even if in innocence, on agriculture and the public that agriculture would go out of business without the use of pesticides.

The San Joaquin Valley is a microcosm of modern world agricultural practices. Where primitive practices are still being used, other factors contribute to soil depletion and agricultural problems. In Africa, for example, people have in the past moved from one agricultural site to another when the soil was depleted. This allowed an average of about eight years for the land to lie fallow before man returned to refarm it. The crush of population has made the lapsed time less and less as man has less space in which to operate. This is true of many other lands where similar nomadic farming is practiced.

The San Joaquin Valley is a clear-cut case of what Barry Commoner has stated as the three basic rules of ecology: (1) Everything is related to everything else; (2) there's no such thing as a free lunch; and (3) everything has to go someplace.

Depletion of agricultural lands, or their despoliation, is resulting from factors other than poor or misguided farming practices. Highways now cover an area the size of Massachusetts, Connecticut, Vermont, Rhode Island, and Delaware. In downtown Los Angeles, 66 percent of the land is taken up by parking lots or streets, and in the entire Los Angeles area, one third of the land is paved. Conservative estimates are that within thirty years something approaching 50 percent of the arable land of California will be under pavement, industry, or housing developments. Considering that California provides approximately 40 percent of the table vegetables, fruits, and nuts for the entire country, this is an alarming prediction. Pessimists, on the other hand, are predicting that by that time 80 percent of the arable land will be gone. The spread of our cities and sprawl of our suburbs claim at least a million and a half acres of open land every year, a 50 percent more rapid depletion than a decade ago. Certainly this is cause for alarm when world population is increasing at a rate far more rapidly than our ability to produce sufficient food.[63] About two tenths of an acre of prime agricultural land is taken out of production all over the United States for each person added to the population. Slurbs and tract housing are far more profitable than agriculture. Investing in agricultural land for the purpose of farming is impractical from a capitalistic point of view.

Many believe that diminishing agricultural land will be offset by increasing harvests with new seeds and better fertilizer, and at the present time worldwide excitement over the so-called Green Revolution would appear to support that belief. As a result of new strains of wheat, rice, and corn, there have been breakthroughs where those engaged in agriculture are sufficiently sophisticated and educated to take advantage of them. At the present time, the result in the wheat market is turmoil. Bumper crops of wheat, chiefly a result of a long period of favorable weather, have upset world wheat-trading. (The devastation to the economy of the Canadian wheat-growing provinces has resulted in farmers bartering their wheat at 25 cents to 45 cents per bushel for necessities.) Even with continuous cooperation from the weather, a quite unlikely event, the Green Revolution will be passed by population within twenty years.

The current wheat glut does not, of course, mean that the hungry of the world are being fed. It simply means that there are nations with wheat surpluses for sale. Of all major wheat growers, the United States alone gives away substantial quantities of wheat. The economy of the other major wheat growers, Canada, Australia, and Argentina, is so closely tied to their agriculture that they cannot afford the same degree of generosity as the United States.[64] Although wheat harvests in Russia and India in the past few years have surpassed expectations, their continued production is undependable because of unreliable weather patterns.

The Green Revolution has been a result of the development of high-yield strains of seed, good weather, irrigation, and chemical fertilizers, and does not diminish the concomitant problems of intensive use of insecticides, irrigation, and chemical fertilizers which have already been examined. Few of the hungry nations of the world can afford, and even if they could, many do not possess, an agriculture sufficiently sophisticated to make use of such farming practices and specialized strains.

Wheat production is not a substantial profit-making venture. Its production throughout the world is subsidized, usually at prices above the world market,[65] but only the United States, where agriculture constitutes a mere 3 percent of the gross national product, can *afford* really substantial subsidies. India and Pakistan, who can ill afford to do so, subsidize their wheat at 100 percent above the world market price. Most of the developing nations of the world are teetering on the edge of bankruptcy much of the time, but without subsidies, agricultural production would decrease with obvious negative consequences.

It is more expensive and more difficult to grow the wonder cereals, and return profits are low. It seems very unlikely that they will, in the long run, do very much to alleviate the world's hunger. Given the present economic structure, people must have money to buy food, no matter how spectacular harvests are. In the United States itself, the richest country in the world, there are some fifteen million people who are hungry because they do not have money for food, an intolerable and inexcusable situation.

In addition to the above disadvantages, the highly touted wonder cereals are considered inferior where they are grown.[66] Not only can they not compete in the world market, in home markets they are generally discounted between 15 percent and 20 percent. Where they have been introduced elsewhere to bolster agriculture they have met with resistance. For example, in Southeast Asia, where many eat their daily rice with their fingers, the complaint about the new Philippine strain is that it is sticky and clings to the fingers. The taste of the new Mexican wheat is not pleasing to the palate of the Afghan, and African bakers have difficulty baking bread with it. It may be possible to change the tastes of peoples, but overcoming the economic facts is quite something else. With the introduction of the new rice strain, the Philippines have been able to export rice, but it has been at a loss because world prices were less than the Philippine government paid its farmers. In addition, the rice was poor in quality and shipping it was expensive. The same problems plague the new Mexican wheat.[67] Despite the temporary advance the Green Revolution has produced, it does not appear that it is the panacea for world hunger.

Inevitably, when the subject of feeding the hungry comes up, someone will bring up the subject of the sea as salvation. Paul Ehrlich, population dynamicist, states, "Perhaps the most pervasive myth of the population-food crisis is that mankind will be saved by harvesting the 'immeasurable riches' of the sea." [68] Analysis by personnel of the Woods Hole Oceanographic Institution in Massachusetts reveals that the maximum sustainable fish yield is approximately 100 million metric tons. This is less than twice the 1967 harvest, and even more optimistic evaluations would not place the harvest more than 150 million metric tons, unless the harvest expanded to include plankton, which does not appear at the present time to be practical. In any event, harvesting plankton would have serious repercussions on stocks of larger food fish. Such an increased fish harvest would not alleviate the food problem. With the present population growth, there would actually be a decline in per capita yield very soon.

There has already been a serious depletion of certain sea creatures as a result of overfishing. Although twice as many whales were harvested in 1966 as in 1933, the oil yield was only about 60 percent of that in 1933 because of the size of the whales caught. The large whales are hovering in the vicinity of extinction. From 1963 to 1964, whalers harvested roughly three times the estimated sustainable yield, according to biological predictions.[69] Fishing is an international enterprise, and little can be done to limit catches and establish uniform, sensible size limits. Many other species are diminishing along with the whale. Overexploited stocks include the East Asian and California sardines, Northwest Pacific salmon, cod, menhaden, tuna in the Atlantic, Pacific, and Indian oceans, and many other valuable food fish throughout the waters of the world. Halibut is under a hemispheric conservation plan. Shellfish, found chiefly in estuaries and bays, are particularly menaced by contaminated water. Oyster harvests, for example, have decreased from 8,070,320 pounds in 1908 to 307,900 pounds in 1950, and further to 160,000 pounds in 1961.[70]

Fishing harvests more than doubled between 1953 and 1967, and international competition is such that the catches will continue to increase until we have destroyed the food yield by overfishing, unless the fishing nations of the world can reach some viable and binding agreement. The outlook is anything but optimistic. It would appear to be a foregone conclusion that as food supplies become more and more critical, the competition is bound to increase. Food from the sea provides comparatively few calories, but it does provide one fifth of the world's protein; three fifths if eggs and milk are omitted. Future stocks are likely to be in jeopardy as long as there are countries such as Japan which depend on their fishing industry to supply one and one half times as much protein as their agricultural production, and are, therefore, critically dependent on seafood.

Walter Prescott Webb in his book *The Great Frontier*, asks the questions: "If you could hold in your right hand the earth in miniature as it was in 1500 or 1600 and in your left hand the earth as it is now, which earth would you consider richer in resources? Or preferable as a desirable base of future operations?" and answers: "On the first earth you would have the Great Frontier, the natural forests, the clear streams, the virgin soils, and the precious metals intact. On the second earth you would have stumps, foul streams, eroded soils, and outside of Kentucky a depleted store of precious metals. As a manager of real estate, applied science has done a bad job and has left the land in a worse state than it found it." [71] Science, and its handmaiden technology, speeded up the rate of destruction of the forests, minerals, soil, and water without creating anything other than the assurance that temporary by-products will cease to be when the destruction of the environment is completed.

The golden land that was once Egypt, with rich fields spreading over it, now spends a shriveled existence in the valley of the Nile. "China, once lush with forests and the fruits of vine and twig, has watched her deserts move in, driving her too fecund people before them into the last refuges of the valleys of the Blue and Yellow Rivers." [72] Under the reign of Solomon, the cedars of Lebanon were decimated for his Temple, and the forest never recovered. The Sahara, which once harbored fertile lands, has been moving southward for five hundred years at about one mile a year on an eighteen-hundred-mile front.

These are case histories of man's advancing technology which has left behind it a long trail of havoc and destruction. The next chapter will take a closer look at some of that destruction.

5

ECOCIDE

Every year a million or so acres fall before the bulldozer and become part of the urban sprawl. Acres of farmland, swamp, field, and forests disappear. Swamps and marshes are filled, hills are leveled, replacing the natural look of the landscape with a product of the engineering mind-set. Highways, airports, houses, streets, sidewalks, factories, warehouses—all rush to claim the land. Trees and grass, hills and streams, are rapidly becoming things confined to areas set aside as nature "museums," where often it is necessary to pay admission to view them. Our landscape is being brutalized by a philosophy which says, "Because it can be built at a profit, it should be built."

This construction mania has produced machinery which literally boggles the mind. There are now earth-moving machines of eighteen thousand horsepower, which are taller than a twenty-story building, longer than a city block, and wider than an eight-lane highway, which are capable of digging two hundred thousand tons of earth per day. At the same time we are building *on,* we are taking out of the earth tons of minerals. Minerals are the very foundation for the sustenance of an industrialized society.

They provide heat and light, construction material, transportation and communication. More minerals have been used in this century than throughout all of previous history, and this usage will not only follow the population curve, but it will increase with man's demand for *more* of the "comforts" of modern civilization.

Consumption of iron ore in 1967 in the United States was about one ton per capita, as compared with 0.17 of a ton for the world as a whole. With a population doubled by 2000, at the same consumption rate, it is apparent that to maintain the present standard of living the use of iron ore will have to be at least doubled. World consumption by that time will be 3.25 billion tons, an increase of six times the present production. Assuming a world population in 2000 of six and a half billion, and an increased standard of living boosting per capita consumption to the present level in the United States of one ton, needs would require twelve times the present production. The story with other minerals is similar. Present United States consumption of copper is eighteen pounds per person as compared with world consumption of three and two tenths pounds per person. To bring world consumption to that of the United States by 2000 would require eleven times the present copper production, or 58.5 million tons, compared with the present 5.25 million tons. Lead consumption in the United States stands at twelve pounds per person; in the world, 1.5 pounds. Thirty-nine million tons would be necessary to make world consumption equivalent to that of the United States, or sixteen times the present output.

Such projections are obviously unrealistic. There are already shortages of silver, mercury, and tin, and all mineral deposits are finite—it is simply a matter of time

before demand exceeds supply.[73] There is no known substitute for a number of minerals on which modern civilization depends. For example, there is no known substitute
for steel, a construction necessity, or cobalt, without
which modern communication would be impossible.

To return to present realities, the United States is almost totally dependent on imports for a great number of
minerals necessary to industry. For example, more than
50 percent of the following minerals are imported: Co-
lumbium and tantalum minerals, industrial diamonds
(100 percent), tin, asbestos (long fiber), platinum, man-
ganese ore, sheet mica, antimony, chromite, cobalt, rutile,
graphite (100 percent), quartz crystal, bismuth, nickel,
bauxite, fluorspar, and lead. Many of these minerals are at
the 75 percent level of importation. They are used in everything imaginable, from the manufacture of surgical
instruments to furnace linings. Without them, our industrial development would cease to be possible.

The average person in the United States under the age
of sixty would find it difficult to learn to live without
highways, telephones, automobiles, to say nothing of such
American "necessities" as typewriters, cameras, television,
radio, tape recorders, electricity, air conditioning, washing
machines, electric mixers, dryers, and dishwashers. The
list, of course, is nearly endless as anyone of the "affluent
society" can prove to himself simply by looking around
his own house or office. In addition to depleting natural
resources to produce these consumer items, the manufacture of each of them results in the production of undesirable by-products which result in air, soil, or water pollution. None, of course, would be possible to manufacture
without the use of electrical power, which is responsible
for air/water chemical, and thermal pollution. The alumi-

num industry alone uses 10 percent of the power production in the United States.[74]

Since power is necessary for the production of all consumer goods, and the average household and business office could scarcely stay in operation without it, it should be fruitful to take a very close look at some of the problems accompanying the production of power, keeping in mind that power consumption is doubling roughly every ten years. Waste heat is one of the serious pollution problems with the production of power. In a power plant, where electricity is produced either by thermonuclear power or the burning of fossil fuels, getting rid of waste heat is one of the necessary steps of production. The use of uranium for production of power produces approximately 60 percent more waste heat than the burning of fossil fuels.[75] For every three units of heat produced in a steam electric utility plant, one unit is used to produce electricity, and two units are discharged as waste.

Other problems connected with power production are far-reaching in consequence. For example, it may seem simpleminded to state that a coal-fired plant needs coal, but it is true, of course, and creates its own problems. If the coal comes from strip-mining, there are many undesirable by-products. Water running over land exposed by strip-mining carries sulfuric acid into rivers and streams, making fish inedible and altering the underwater ecology. Where strip-mining is prevalent and regulations slack, whole communities have suffered from landslides and erosion. Sometimes houses are simply washed down hillsides. Deforestation and slag piles are other by-products. If the coal comes from underground mines, the health and safety hazards are well known. Once the coal is mined, it must be transported to the power plant. In the cases where this is transported by truck or train, additional heat waste and other pollutants are generated. In the case of oil as fuel being carried by pipeline, energy and metal were used for its construction.

The problem of thermal pollution has only recently become a matter of grave concern, with the tremendous increase in the need for electrical power. Waste heat introduced into any natural body of water results in changes in the aquatic life.[76] Some forms of aquatic life die, some become more susceptible to disease, successful spawning is decreased, and mortality in the young increases; migration patterns are altered; relationships between prey and predator are altered; oxygen content of the water is reduced; rooted plant growth increases, which alters the flow rate and results in increased siltation where it is not natural. In addition, because of the difference between night and day power demands, the temperature of the water often fluctuates rapidly, to which fish are extremely sensitive. Not merely the aquatic life is affected. Changes are necessary for the purification of water for human consumption when the temperature of the water is increased. Sometimes recreational use of the water must be abandoned.

To gain a perspective on the dimension of the problem, note the following: In February, 1970, Walter Hickel, Secretary of the Interior, threatened court action against the Florida Power and Light Company concerning construction of a cooling canal designed to release heated water into Biscayne Bay from two nuclear generators under construction. When both are in operation sometime in 1972, five and one half billion gallons of heated water would be dumped *daily* into the lower end of the Bay. Hot water produced by the present conventional plant has already killed all plant life in a 550-acre section of the Bay. As presently projected, by the year 2000, power plants will dispose of enough waste heat to raise the temperature in all surface waters of the United States by twenty degrees.[77]

In addition to thermal pollution, and coincidental chemical by-products which pollute air and water, polluting chemicals are deliberately added to water used in steam electric utility plants to protect the machinery, prevent accumulation of slime, and control the acidity of the water. None of these chemicals is recovered or removed from the waste dumped, and some of them render fish toxic for human consumption.

Further, every mile of transmission line can eat up at least fifty acres of land, and thus long distances from the consumer increase the amount of land used. On the other hand, proximity of power plants to large population centers increases the possibility of exposure to pollution—chemical, thermal, or radioactive.

Early hopes for production of cheap power from nuclear fission have been frustrated. By 1968, only seventeen civilian and one military nuclear power plants had been built. Five of these had been shut down as unsafe or impractical; another never operated properly, and was finally put out of business altogether by an accident. A seventh has been kept in safe operation only by reduced power production. The balance have had various difficulties, and an eighth was shut down in 1969.[78]

Production of cheap power from nuclear fission produced the anticipation that about half of our power, by the year 2000, would be nuclear power. At the present time, this appears to be merely wishful thinking for a number of reasons. In the first place, according to the experts, there will be a shortage of available uranium by 1980, and a severe shortage ten years later.[79] The only possible solution apparent at the present time is the development of "breeder" reactors, that is, reactors which can convert Uranium 238, not fissionable, into a usable fuel. According to Glen Seaborg, chairman of the Atomic Energy Commission, in an address made in 1968, it will require about 250,000 tons of refined uranium ore to supply the necessary fuel for nuclear plants in the next ten years, but the supply which is economically recoverable amounts only to 148,000 tons.[80]

In addition to thermal problems, operating problems, and shortages of fuel, there is the problem of continual radiation danger during operation and the disposal of radioactive waste. Dr. Edward Teller has made the following statement concerning the safety hazards involved in thermonuclear power production:

> A single major mishap in a nuclear reactor could cause extreme damage, not because of the explosive force, but because of the radioactive contamination. . . . So far we have been extremely lucky. . . . But with the spread of industrialization, with the greater number of simians monkeying around with things that they do not completely understand, sooner or later a fool will prove greater than the proof even in the foolproof system.[81]

An atomic reactor electrical power plant is an exceedingly complex and delicate piece of machinery, far more than is generally realized. Errors of operation or failures of equipment which would be quite minor in a conventional plant could easily result in loss of life or even total destruction of a nuclear plant. The most dangerous possibility is an explosion that would result in the escape of substantial amounts of radioactive material. Even in the small plants now operating such accidents have occurred several times, and only blind luck has precluded significant loss of life. In the large plants anticipated in the 1970's, the radioactive hazard from an explosion could kill all life in an area from one to ten miles wide and from thirty to fifty or more miles long, depending upon wind direction and velocity. Such an accident could kill millions of people and cause literally tens of billions of dollars worth of property damage. (NOTE: Liability for this kind of damage has been limited by congressional action to a maximum of $500 million, no matter what the actual damage might be.)

For those who feel sure that modern technology can guarantee the safety of complex machinery, a look at the space program is worthwhile. Throughout history there has not been a more carefully engineered operation than our space program, using the most skilled scientists and engineers, and yet, despite the care, there have been three major failures resulting from faulty materials and carelessness. The public is well aware of these major failures in the United States, and we can only surmise that Russia has surely had at least an equal number of failures. In the United States, there was the death of the three astronauts during a flight "rehearsal," while still on the launching pad; the foolish launching of a ship during an electrical storm (simply in order that the President might witness takeoff), resulting in a fortunately brief but total electrical power failure, when it was struck by lightning; and the explosion resulting from faulty insulation on a pump in an oxygen tank which crippled Apollo 13's intended moon shot, but luckily did not result in the loss of lives. These major catastrophes occurred in a program operating under the most skilled personnel. There have been, of course, numerous lesser accidents resulting in the loss of equipment.

Reliance on technology appears even more hazardous when considering the F-111, which is admittedly a much less complicated machine than a spaceship. Yet, after five or six years of development, and an expenditure estimated at $11.2 billion, the F-111 had to be phased out because it could not be made to perform satisfactorily, or even comparatively safely.

The personnel constructing a nuclear power plant consist of such people as pipe fitters and electricians, who, even though they may be perfectly capable technicians, obviously do not understand the intricate and unbelievably complicated problems inherent in thermonuclear physics. Industrial accidents happen all the time in every field of industry, but what might be a routine accident in a steel foundry can easily be a fatal accident in a nuclear-powered utility plant. For example, a cut finger, people bumping into each other, a leaky pipe, a spilled container, a dropped glass tube, are accidents that would be considered "serious" by the Atomic Energy Commission.[82] With operation so delicate and serious, it is imperative that personnel be highly skilled and thoroughly trained. That this is not always true is pointed out by Curtis and Hogan with the following incident. In 1964, a man employed by United Nuclear Corporation was asked to rock a plastic container, five inches in diameter and sixty inches high, on his shoulder to bring about a desired chemical mixture of radioactive material and then to decant it into a container eighteen inches in diameter and twenty-six inches high. The latter container concentrated the material into a critical mass. A runaway chain reaction resulted, and the man, untrained in the field of chemistry or thermonuclear physics, was unprepared for the explosive reaction. He was spattered with the material and was dead two days later.[83]

Annual reports of the Atomic Energy Commission to Congress read like a physicists' nightmare.[84] A major disaster has not yet occurred, but with the proliferation of nuclear plants expected and human error ineradicable, it would appear to be merely a matter of time. A peaceful labor walkout in a plant that *must* be manned around the clock could result in such a disaster. It takes very little imagination to contemplate a possible terrifying calamity. There is no reason to believe that workers in a nuclear power plant are any less human than those in other kinds of plants. For example, duplicate in a nuclear plant the following problems that have occurred in a conventional plant. In 1966, a contract between twenty-four hundred members of the International Brotherhood of Electrical Workers and the Alabama Power Company broke down. Within thirteen days saboteurs opened oil valves at four substations, draining an essential coolant from the transformers. Within three months there were forty-five acts of sabotage. Office personnel replaced plant personnel, that is, when they could get through the plant picket lines. Any one of the acts of sabotage could result in a serious accident in a nuclear plant.[85]

Barring an accident or sabotage, normal leakage and intentional release of radioactive material can cause critical hazards in the next few years. The problem is partly caused by the fact that many of the radioactive compounds which are released have a lengthy lifetime and their effect is cumulative. For example, strontium 90, which accumulates in the bone structure, has a half life of twenty-seven years. Thus, even though these long-lived isotopes may be widely dispersed, their radioactivity can continue to accumulate.

Radioactive materials can concentrate in plant and animal life. In a study of water in the Columbia River, it was discovered that while the radioactivity of the water was insignificant, the radioactivity of the river plankton was two thousand times greater.[86] The radioactivity of the fish and ducks feeding on the plankton was fifteen thousand and forty thousand times greater, respectively. The radioactivity of young swallows, fed on insects caught by their parents in the river, was five hundred thousand times greater, and the radioactivity of the egg yolks of water birds was more than a million times greater. What must be kept in mind is that the greater concentrations of radioactivity occur at the higher levels of the food chain.

After studying all aspects of the production of atomic reactor energy, Curtis and Hogan conclude that in this matter we have made a colossal error and that we should forthwith "proceed with the complete abandonment of the nuclear power plant program." [87] They say nothing could be more insane than to continue the erection of this threat of incredible magnitude to the human race. Lest these authors be written off as scaremongers or their findings be regarded as insignificant, it would be well to consider the statement on the frontispiece of the book made by the former chairman of AEC, David Lilienthal:

Far and away the most comprehensive and sensible statement ever made about the hazards and limitations of atomic power. Once a bright hope shared by all mankind, myself included, the rash proliferation of atomic power plants has become one of the ugliest clouds overhanging America. . . . This book will have to be answered, soberly and persuasively, by those responsible for this proliferation.

Finally, there is the problem of the disposal of radio-active wastes. Some of these must be shipped from the eastern seaboard plants to a disposal site in the state of Washington, three thousand miles away. In order to accomplish this, special containers must be made which will withstand possible mishandling or accidents during the journey.[88] Storage is of necessity planned for centuries, since the life of radioactive wastes exceeds six hundred years, but already some tanks are leaking and must be replaced. According to Ritchie Calder, in *Living with the Atom,* projected power production by nuclear reactors in the year 2000 would mean that the amount of fission products on highways would be nine hundred eighty million curies! He regards this as a "mighty lot of curies roaming around a populated country." Highway accidents, container damage, piracy, sabotage, accidental loss—all of these have occurred, and will continue to occur as long as fissionable materials must be transported from one place to another.

There is also the problem of the long-term exposure of a great number of people to low levels of radiation during normal operation and from all sources in modern life. If, as predicted by the AEC, power generation in the United States by the year 2000 is about equally divided between fossil fuel and nuclear plants, radiation levels may be high enough to affect seriously all living things, unless some startling and unforeseen innovation in controlling radioactive effluents appears.

The radiation problems from the production of nuclear

power *at the present time*, however, are insignificant compared to the air pollution problems from steam electric utility plants burning fossil fuels. They contribute pollutants to water or air consisting of sulfur dioxide, carbon dioxide, particulate matter (one fourth of total), nitrogen oxides, hydrocarbons, and of course, the waste heat mentioned earlier.[89] Adding the loss of valuable land, we are paying a very high price for the use of electricity. Assuming fossil fuel plants comprise one half the total by the year 2000, they will be emitting 8.75 billion tons of carbon dioxide per year. This, added to increased water vapor, could completely alter the earth's climate.[90]

Sulfur dioxide emissions, whatever their source (utility plants contribute approximately one half the total), have been medically associated with respiratory disease. It is disquieting to note that emphysema, once considered the disease of elderly people, particularly male smokers, now ranks as second for Social Security disability benefits. For the first time, infants are being treated for emphysema. Incidence of the disease has doubled every five years since World War II. In the last year of record, thirty thousand deaths were attributed to it and it was related to approximately sixty thousand more.[91] All the while sulfur remains a mere waste in sulfur dioxide emissions, we continue to mine each year several million tons of sulfur. Depletion and waste have become the twin tragedies of the modern industrial state.

The capacity of water, land, and air to sustain the damage from power production cannot sustain a doubling of that power every ten years. As far as land is concerned, utility companies are already faced with a real lack of suitable site locations. Consolidated Edison in New York has been trying unsuccessfully for several years to build a thermonuclear plant on the Hudson River north of New York City. As a matter of fact, they have been prevented from building any new plants since the mid-1960's. The proposed plant on the Hudson has been blocked by conservation groups and local residents who do not wish to pay for power with the negative benefits that accompany its production and location. Yet the citizens of New York have been warned that there is a serious power shortage in the East already, and they face either the likelihood of a brownout or the possibility of another disastrous blackout such as occurred in November, 1965.

So far, the discussion has been limited to electric power plants run on fossil fuels or nuclear energy. Now it is time to look at the problems concomitant with the use of falling water to produce power, which in the United States amounts to about 14 percent of the total production. Hydroelectric power production avoids the pollution problems mentioned above, but creates problems of its own. Since there are few natural falls in the United States, the major portion of hydroelectric power is produced by the impounding of water behind dams built to create an artificial "fall." Dam projects inevitably produce far-reaching environmental problems over vast amounts of land. As has been examined with relation to the Aswân Dam in Egypt, resulting phenomena are not even predictable. Effects, other than those examined in Chapter 3 on land use, are often not well known by the general public. For example, the water table of a vast area may rise as a result of impounding a large volume of water. As with water seepage from irrigation canals, these rising waters carry with them the mineral deposits in the soil. This often results in altering large areas of agricultural land, making it difficult to cultivate, and can result in poisoning domestic water supplies. The growth of aquatic plants behind a dam can result in insufficient water flow for the production of electricity.

More often than not, a dam is built without any prior environmental or sociological survey. At least for one proposed dam development project, however, a fairly thorough study has been made, and some of the predicted repercussions are not encouraging. Currently, there is a plan to develop the Mekong Delta in southeast Asia into an Oriental TVA. The plan carries with it the hope of fruitful negotiations with North Vietnam by promising food, water, and electrical power. This plan would dam the largest remaining undammed, unbridged river in the world.[92] In a study made for the Agency for International Development, the following warnings were sounded: Altogether, seven hundred thousand people would have to be resettled (precipitating what Dr. Richard Van Cleve, dean of the College of Fisheries, University of Washington, has termed "a major debacle"); some of those resettled would be removed from rich lowland rice paddies to hilly regions with poor soil, requiring irrigation, fertilizer, improved seeds and pesticides (the fertilizer and pesticides will pollute the river); floods would spread disease-carrying snails which flourish in the steady water provided by irrigation; DDT, or other pesticides, would kill new pests, kill off the cat population, precipitate a rat explosion (a phenomenon that has already occurred several times in various places), which would damage the harvests, and everyone would be worse off than before. They supposedly would be compensated because their misery would be lighted by electricity.

Displaced populations are often subject to new strains of disease, such as malaria. This problem occurred in northern Thailand where people were forced to move to the hills and a new strain of malaria struck. This was combated by the use of DDT to kill the offending mosquitoes. The cat population, unfortunately, was killed off, leaving a free field behind for a rat invasion.

The two planned new reservoirs in the Mekong, according to David Challinor, director of the Office of International Activities of the Smithsonian Institution, would flood some of the best hardwood stands and cotton-producing land in Thailand, in addition to the loss of the rice land. And, as in any dam project, impounding water in one region may deny ample water to another, and as the Rienows point out, big dams are really only a temporary expedient for local retention of water. Storage capacity often must be increased to ensure an adequate flow of water, and increased storage is sometimes canceled by evaporation. Lake Mead, for example, loses seven vertical feet of water to evaporation each year. And, inevitably, dams always silt up, becoming what the Rienows call "useless monuments to ugliness." [93]

There has not as yet been a study of the effect of the Mekong plan on fishing in the area. Fish are the major source of protein for the Delta. If the project goes through, the effects on the fish are certain to be extensive, and likely to be negative. There have been a number of studies of the effects of the erection of dams on fish, unfortunately after the fact. The beaver complex of the Army Corps of Engineers has been responsible for the near elimination of Pacific salmon, Atlantic salmon, sturgeon, and blue-shaded shad, among others.

The effects of damming rivers show very clearly in studies of the Columbia River in the West. There is only one fifty-mile stretch of free-flowing water left on the Columbia River, from the United States tidewater to the

Canadian border, and the Corps is anxious to span this with the Ben Franklin Dam, at a cost, by the way, of approximately $300 million, which would take one hundred years to pay for itself. This would obliterate the last natural flow of river, add to the interdam mortality of the salmon and complete the destruction of the natural ecology.[94]

Seven different varieties of salmon have through the years used the Columbia and its tributaries for spawning grounds. In the eighteenth century, and before, salmon supported an extensive Indian culture. In the lower estuary of the river, and inland, the Indians would catch salmon on their annual runs, which they would then dry for their own use and for purposes of trade. In the late 1800's and early 1900's, the summer chinook catch alone was more than forty million pounds per year. Today, there are four Army Corps of Engineers dams backing each other up. They are joined by five public utility dams, which are in turn backed up by two more Army Corps dams, culminating in the Grand Coulee. Except for the one stretch of fifty miles, all main-stem Columbia River salmon spawning areas have been obliterated by inundation.[95] Tens of thousands of adult fish die every year attempting to reach their upstream spawning grounds, despite fish ladders and motorized transportation at some locations, which are very expensive. In 1965, it was estimated that more than 70 percent of the entire run of spring chinook headed for the tributaries above Bonneville Dam (that nearest tidewater) perished, and for the first time in history the salmon fishing season was closed on the Snake River and its tributaries.

In addition to fish loss from dams, in the past ten years the United States has lost 135 million fish because of water pollution. In May, 1970, on the Missouri River alone, approximately four hundred thousand fish were lost because of a pollution accident and a criminal disregard for handling deadly poisons.[96] Despite efforts to save the salmon on the Columbia, the catch was down to seventeen million pounds as compared with forty-nine million pounds in 1911.[97]

On the other side of the continent, the Aroostook River in Maine was once considered among the finest rivers for salmon spawning in the United States. Now, seventy dams straddle it or its tributaries. End of story. End of salmon! The Maine salmon catch, amounting to one hundred fifty thousand pounds in 1889, was fewer than one thousand pounds by 1950. Commercial fishing is practically non-existent and sport fishing an "expensive excursion into nostalgia." [98] The sturgeon catch on the East Coast of 1.2 million pounds in 1897 had dwindled to twenty-five thousand pounds in 1961; of forty-nine million pounds of blue-shaded shad once caught up and down the East Coast, the supply has gone down to eight million pounds.[99]

Through a chain of events triggered by thermal pollution at a nuclear power plant at Indian Point on the Hudson River, an estimated two million bass were lost. Accurate counts were prevented by secrecy. Fish were hauled away, buried with lime to speed decomposition; fish kills were guarded by hired Burns detectives. A naturalist, making a private investigation, reported seeing twelve-foot-high mounds of dead bass being bulldozed into pits, as a run of trucks hauled in more. He reported an estimated ten thousand dead fish under the Indian Point power station docks.[100]

The Columbia and Aroostook Rivers are only two of hundreds of rivers that have been turned into a series of reservoirs, and as cited above, dams are only one of the ways in which we are destroying our fish. Someone has said, "This is the most dammed country on earth!" Ah! But we have electricity to run electric toothbrushes, can openers, knives, pencil sharpeners, combs, scissors, hair curlers, and to manufacture what appears to be destined to become the most permanent littering device invented by ingenious man—the aluminum can.

Consideration of power production and usage has been confined to the United States, without mentioning the sheer catastrophe of producing power for worldwide consumption at a level approaching that in the United States. The capacity of the biosphere to absorb the waste by-products of electric power generation will soon be reached. In any event, the earth cannot go on indefinitely providing sufficient fuel for increasing production of power. Already, low sulfur coal, needed for the production of electricity because it emits less sulfur dioxide, is erratic in supply and expensive in cost. Coal is not, of course, the chief source for all energy, but it is the chief fuel for electric power, and when oil and natural gas are long gone, we will look to coal as the fuel for future production of power. Presently, coal supplies 51 percent of power fuel; natural gas, 23 percent; oil, 10 percent; uranium, 1½ percent; and hydroelectric power the rest.[101]

The United States annual consumption of oil, our chief source of all energy, jumped from forty million barrels in 1900 to three billion barrels in the 1960's, and projections place the consumption at twelve billion barrels by the year 2000. That is a total of 300 billion barrels of oil! The projection reveals that in the last three years of the twentieth century, consumption would be the same as that for the entire first half of the century.[102] No one can predict with a high degree of accuracy just how long the supply of gas and oil will last—what can be predicted with certainty is that the supplies are limited and, historically speaking, will be depleted soon. Within less than one hundred years it is predicted that available supplies of both will be inadequate for projected needs.[103] By 2000, we will still be burning coal, the dirtiest fuel, largely to produce electricity. Whether coal, oil, gas, or uranium are the chief source of energy for production of power, it seems certain that hydroelectric power will not play a major role, which means that something like 95 percent of our power supply will come from nonrenewable sources.[104] Depletion of resources, soil and its products, is becoming an increasing problem in an industrialized world.

Power plants are not the only villains producing noxious gases that pollute the air. They are not even the chief ones. Sulfur dioxide, however, of which they are the chief single source, has been implicated in all of the severe episodes of air pollution. There have been five major publicized air disasters in the past forty years.[105] In the London episode of 1952, forty-five hundred people died in a ten-day period from immediate effects, and an estimated ten thousand died subsequently from delayed effects. In Donora, Pennsylvania, one third of the entire population of the town became ill from a smog trapped by a thermal inversion. Statistical analysis of a 1953 inversion in New York, revealed 260 "excess" deaths in one day, apparently directly related to an unusually high level of sulfur dioxide in the air.[106]

Although there are no studies linking higher infant mortality and a short life-span among blacks in urban areas to the higher air pollution levels found there, such a statistical correlation warrants suspicion. The housing of the urban poor is usually closer to heavy industry, more prevalent with old, and thus inefficient automobiles with high pollutant emissions, and finally, subject to the daily influx of commuters in still more automobiles en route to the urban center. Dwellers in urban areas are certain to be seriously affected by air pollution. At the present rate of buildup of pollutants in the air, thousands of deaths will undoubtedly occur in the coming years as a direct result, and many lives will be shortened and subject to diseases related to exposure.

As mentioned above, power plants or other industrial enterprises are not the major air polluters. So much, however, has been said and written about the role the automobile plays in the picture that there is little left to say which would not be redundant. Henry Ford's four-wheeled monster is responsible for something like 70 percent of all pollutants in the air, and for the fact that 90 percent of the carbon monoxide in the atmosphere is concentrated in the northern hemisphere. The automobile is responsible for contributing to the air carbon monoxide, nitrogen oxides, hydrocarbons, lead, asbestos, and other particulate matter. The smog hanging over cities comes chiefly from automobile emissions. All the pollutants put into the air from automobiles are harmful, in one way or another, to plant and animal life, including man.

As a matter of fact, all emissions from automobiles, industry, domestic, and municipal sources are harmful to life, and may result in consequences completely unforeseen. Dust fall in the average city is equal to approximately fifteen tons per square mile per month, but in a city such as New York it can run as high as thirty tons per square mile per month, as recorded in 1969.[107] Particulate matter, along with carbon dioxide and water vapor, can scatter sunlight, reducing the amount of energy reaching the earth, or in combination can concentrate heat from the sun in a greenhouse effect, raising the temperature of the atmosphere.

Increased amounts of carbon dioxide will undoubtedly have serious effects on the earth's climate. The average global temperature has dropped 0.2 percent since 1945. About 31 percent of the earth's surface is cloud covered. An increase to 36 percent would drop the temperature four degrees centigrade—sufficient to precipitate a new ice age.[108] With the introduction of water vapor and carbon dioxide from the SST, above atmospheric turbulence or precipitation, only science fiction can picture possible repercussions on world climate. Consumption of fuel for air travel has increased from 1940 to 1967, from 22 million gallons to 512 million gallons annually, seeding an already threatened atmosphere with additional gases.[109] Our fuel-burning has raised the carbon dioxide level in the atmosphere 10 percent in the past one hundred years, and anticipated future use may increase the level by 25 percent by the year 2000.

If, as some fear, accumulation of carbon dioxide in the atmosphere results in the "greenhouse" effect, the earth will face an entirely new agenda of problems. While it might increase some agricultural production, it would decrease dairy products. Cattle cannot increase evaporative cooling with increasing environmental temperature and they develop a fever when the temperature rises above 80 degrees Fahrenheit. This firmly establishes them in the temperate zone, along with most of the rest of agriculture. The rise in cattle temperature results in decrease of milk production.[110]

Robert Rienow has estimated that, at the present rate,

50 percent of the sunlight will be cut off from the earth by 1985. According to the Smithsonian Institution, the sunlight reaching Washington has decreased by 16 percent in the last few years. Dr. Alfred Hulstrunk at the Atmospheric Science Research Center states that we have hung a veil of dirty air over the cities and much of our countryside which has cut off 20 percent of the sunlight.[111] If the buildup is allowed to continue, the "global gloom" will not be reversible. It will not be like the massive emergency situations of London or Donora which were weather triggered; it will be a permanent alteration of *climate,* and concern for man will have to be extended to the total environment—plants, animals, water, carnivores, and herbivores—in short, to all the things that keep man alive.[112]

There is a bumper sticker around which asks, "Have You Thanked a Green Plant Today?" Most people would thank a green plant for providing oxygen, which for reasons too involved to discuss, is not entirely accurate. The real reason why we should thank a green plant is that the plant can perform a miracle of which man is absolutely incapable, but which is absolutely essential to the sustenance of all life, and that is the capability of converting the energy from the sun into carbohydrates and oxygen, which is known as photosynthesis. Without the sun, there would be no plant life, either on land or in the seas, and without the energy furnished by plant life, all life would cease to be. Our usual concern is with the economic cost of pollution to agriculture, metal, fabric, paint, and health, but our real concern should be with the endangering of the photosynthetic cycle.

The economic concerns are real enough, of course. According to the Rienows, air pollution has practically decimated the spinach industry in New Jersey, and threatened many other agricultural crops. Connecticut tobacco, used chiefly for cigar wrappers, brings five to six dollars per pound until air pollution enters the picture. Just a fleck of ozone on a tobacco leaf will drop the price to twenty cents.[113] Ozone is a form of oxygen which is peculiarly active and destructive, and which is responsible for ozone "alerts" in Los Angeles when school children are warned to avoid out-of-door exercise. Citrus crops grown in clean air are twice the size of those grown in the kind of air surrounding metropolitan areas. Florists everywhere are suffering extensive crop damage. It is impossible, for example, to grow orchids anywhere near California metropolitan areas. Flowers are one thing, and it would be a drab world without their existence, but the nitty-gritty of the matter is that because of air pollution, despite commercial fertilizers, pesticides, and irrigation, the earth is becoming less productive.

The Atmospheric Science Research Center reports that the pollution funnels are traveling great distances and can settle anywhere, including mountains and valleys. The trees around Lake Arrowhead, ninety miles from Los Angeles, and fifty-one hundred feet high, are dying from Los Angeles produced smog.[114] Approximately 50 percent of the mature pine trees in the San Bernardino National Forest show smog damage; 15 percent are severely damaged and 3 percent are already dead. One thousand acres of afflicted pines fell before the ax in the spring of 1970. Altogether, it is estimated that 1,298,000 trees are affected.

Not merely California trees are victims; the white pines in Tennessee and in the Great Lakes area are affected. The second growth of what was once an impressive forest of white pines are stunted dwarfs. Smog damage is evident in at least twenty states. The entire globe is affected. Tokyo has smog so dense that the blue sky is gone. Black snow and nitrate-laden rain and snow are ruining the forests and streams of Norway. Air that is hostile to forests is also hostile to human beings and animals, but not merely the death of the forests themselves is involved. Subsequent damage included the desiccation of watersheds, the erosion of soils, the threat of fire in stands of dead trees, the problem of floods and mud slides—these are but a few accompanying phenomena.[115]

The Rienows quote the ecologist R. St. Barbe Baker, from his book, *Sahara Challenge,* who equates the skin of the earth with the skin of a burn victim. Doctors know that if a person loses one third of his skin, he dies. Botanists know the same of a tree and its bark. The world now has nine billion acres of desert—earth which has been stripped of her green skin—just short one billion acres of the critical one third, and in the United States alone urban sprawl and highways claim a million acres per year.

Alarm is slow to strike the average person, who worries only about the pollution he can see, and yet to worry about visible air pollution is to be concerned with less than 2 percent of the problem. If we must wait to act until the earth is shrouded in a pall of black smoke, such as Black Tuesday in St. Louis in November, 1939, it will long since have been too late. The problem is concentrated chiefly in the temperate zones, the home of practically all food production, and is affecting not only plants and animals directly with harmful airborne substances, but it is beginning to affect climate patterns, cloud formation, and rainfall.

Air is only one element vital to survival of plant and

animal life; our water is threatened indirectly because of our prodigious demand for energy. Oil spillage in our waters and oceans has become frightening. After the Torrey Canyon disaster, 5,711 oiled birds were cleaned off, and only 150 returned to health and were released; of these, 37 died within a month. Few of the 1,500 diving birds affected recovered. The effect of twelve thousand tons of detergent put into the sea to counteract the effect of the oil was worse than the oil itself—it destroyed marine organic life, and no one knows when or if it will return. Your local service station and its 210,000 counterparts on every corner in the land have the task of getting rid of 350 million gallons of used motor oil annually. Because of packaging and tax laws, it is not profitable to recycle used oil. Most of this ends up in the city sewer via a service station rest room. The Buffalo and Cuyahoga Rivers in New York and Ohio are so badly polluted with oil and waste material that they constitute a fire hazard, and the Cuyahoga has already caught fire and burned down two railroad trestles, causing some $50,000 damage.

Studying water pollution resulting from sources other than oil is, to say the least, a gloomy task. Just to mention the most familiar tragedy—Lake Erie is gone. To save it from *further* pollution would cost in the neighborhood of $10 billion. Nothing lives in it now but trash fish, blood and sludge worms, and bloodsuckers.[116] Phosphates from industrial wastes and urban sewage have killed it. Lake Michigan is sick. "Polluted Water—No Swimming" signs are posted up and down the shore of its public beaches. Oil, debris, slime, and dead fish contaminate the shore. The Chicago shoreline stinks. Boats empty ballast, bilge water, raw sewage, garbage, litter, and oil into the lakes and the St. Lawrence Seaway. Industries dump waste chemicals into the lakes. Farther north in Canada, Lake

St. Clair has been closed to fishing because mercury levels in the water from industrial waste have made the fish unsafe to eat. Potentially dangerous quantities of mercury have been found in waste products from five manufacturing plants on the Lower Mississippi River. The Mississippi provides drinking water for millions of people, and since few water treatment plants touch chemicals, the kidney is left to do all the filtering.

Altering natural waterways can produce the most unforeseen consequences. In Lake Michigan, in sharp contrast to the situation previous to the opening of the St. Lawrence Seaway, 90 percent (poundwise) of the fish are now alewife, a member of the herring family. Not being indigenous to the lake, and having no natural predators there, it simply dies, and mounds of dead carcasses pile up on the beaches, creating a crucial health hazard, to say nothing of a revolting stench. Construction along the shores of any body of water will result in drainage of silt, causing additional problems. Lake Superior is turning into Lake Inferior. Lake Tahoe is threatened. One third of the lakes and streams in the United States are well on the way to a fate similar to Lake Erie's through accelerated eutrophication, and the ever-growing menace to the seas has reached an alarming proportion.

The oyster harvest has been mentioned earlier. It is only one of many varieties of shellfish, which live principally in estuaries, that are endangered or have disappeared. Even where they have managed to survive, they have become toxic to man because they accumulate pollution poisons such as insecticides, poisonous chemicals, and radioactivity. Many large bays and gulfs are seriously endangered by pollution. The Gulf of Mexico is a good example, as it has for years been forced to receive two thirds of the nation's sewage. Not merely gulfs and bays are vulnerable. The fragile fabric of the entire ocean is threatened as we continue to pour pollutants into our waters, and they in turn are dispersed by currents throughout the world.

Dead fish, shellfish, and sea birds were recently washed up along a two-hundred-mile stretch of shoreline in the Pensacola, Florida, area. Investigation revealed heavy concentrations of DDT, although none was used in the Gulf. The source of the DDT was traced to beach-spraying to control dog flies. The DDT washed out on tides or was washed off the spraying instruments which were cleaned in the Gulf waters. Runoff of pesticides used to kill mosquitoes along the Florida and Texas coastlines has resulted in shrimp kills in bait pens along the coast. One such kill in an estuary resulted in depletion of 60 percent of South Carolina's shrimp catch. Our pesticides, crude as they are, are designed to combat arthropods (insects, arachnids, and crustaceans), those creatures with joined feet and limbs, segmented bodies, and horny skeletons. It is unfortunate that lobster, crab, and shrimp fall into this category.[117]

Residues of DDT have been found in the fatty tissues of animals in the Antarctic, where no pesticides have been used. They presumably were airborne and deposited in rain and snow falls. Contrary to insects, which have the ability to develop strains resistant to pesticides, these animals pass pesticides along the reproductive line and survivors have proved more sensitive to them than their parents. Both the North Atlantic and Pacific Oceans are receiving rains of lead from automobile exhausts at the rate of five hundred thousand tons annually. Lead is one of the oceans' rarest minerals and the introduction of it and such poisonous minerals as mercury can completely wreck the ecology of the seas.[118]

The Atomic Energy Commission has for years considered the oceans as the logical dump for radioactive wastes, and they have been deposited in the most thoughtless and careless manner imaginable—for example, in used oil drums weighted with cement. These drums have been accidentally retrieved by fishermen far from the dumping sites, and beachcombers on the coast of Oregon have come across a washed-up drum marked "Atomic Energy Commission—DANGER—Radioactive Material." [119] Sea creatures, being unable to read, go unprotected by the warning. Piped radioactive wastes from nuclear power plants render seabeds and marine plants radioactive.

In June, 1969, approximately forty million fish died in the Rhine River in Germany, and there have been no salmon in the Thames in two hundred years. Most rivers and lakes of northern Italy are devoid of life. The fish sales in Detroit during the spring of 1970 were depleted by 40 percent because of pollution.[120] Lakes Geneva, Constance, and Neuchâtel in Switzerland are so polluted with urban and industrial waste that their trout and perch are nearly gone. The fjords of Norway literally stink with drifting waste.

Increasing oil spills, already mentioned, pump accidents, and pumping neglect compound the problem. Sea birds are particularly vulnerable to oil spills. One oil spill in the North Sea proved fatal to more than two hundred thousand waterfowl, and at least ten thousand pelicans, gulls, grebes, loons, scoters, and swans succumbed to a slick from an oil tanker collision off of San Francisco. On the coast of Newfoundland, over a two-year period, the death of two hundred fifty thousand auks nearly wiped out the entire colony. Lubricated beaches are becoming increasingly common.[121] Accidental or intentional dumping is not limited to chemicals and petroleum; everything from obsolete rocket engines to narcotic contraband end up in the oceans, and plain ordinary sewage outfalls are common on all coasts.

Even our attempts to clean up our water can have disastrous consequences. Primary and secondary treatment purify water to a limited extent, but they do not remove toxic viruses. They convert organic wastes into inorganic compounds such as nitrates and phosphates, and these are added to those already present in the water. These compounds fertilize the streams, prodigious growth of algae follow, and the subsequent death and decomposition deprive the water of necessary oxygen for aquatic life. As a result, the water "dies." Lake Erie is in an advanced state of the eutrophication process, speeded up wherever water from primary or secondary sewage plants is pumped into streams, rivers, or lakes.

Not the least of the problems of modern industrial society is that of solid waste disposal. It is difficult not to agree with the statement, "Technology is a system for manufacturing the need for more technology. When this is combined with an economic system whose major goal is growth, the result is a society in which conspicuous production of garbage is the highest social value." [122] The sewer, the garbage truck, the incinerator, and the dump are, in the long run, the ultimate monuments of the modern industrial state. Treatment of our wastes is perhaps the least thoughtful and sophisticated aspect of our technology.

Throughout urban history man has used his streets and streams to dispose of his garbage. Instead of tossing our garbage out the most convenient window, as in earlier times, it is now carried away in pipes or trucks. We have filled swamps and bays with it. We have filled quarries with it. We have tamped it and burned it. San Francisco has filled approximately one third of the Bay with it, and is looking into plans to ship its garbage and wastes to dumps in the Nevada desert.[123] Space for dumping is critical around every major American metropolis, and incineration has come steadily under criticism in urban communities because of air pollution.

Recycling our wastes, from paper to junked automobiles, is practiced scarcely at all. Of the billion pounds of paper used each year, only about one third is recycled. Nine million cars are abandoned each year, and very few of them are reclaimed as scrap. Each year we junk 100 million tires, 20 million tons of paper, 28 billion bottles, and 48 billion cans. It costs us $2.8 billion simply to collect the garbage. With 6 percent of the world's population, the United States is responsible for nearly 50 percent of the world's pollution.[124] We have become what Garrett DeBell has described as "a nation knee-deep in garbage, firing rockets at the moon." [125]

Our wastes are, of course, tied inexorably to our industrial production—produce, use, discard. Industrialized man has been dazzled by the seemingly limitless flow of finished products, made from raw materials that have to come from somewhere. Developing nations everywhere are anxious to follow the example of the Western world and become industrial nations, often at the expense of vitally needed agricultural products. Conspicuous consumption followed by instant obsolescence, with the attendant waste of resources, has been set forth by us as the pattern all nations should follow for a better future.

Until about 1940, the United States was a "surplus" nation producing more raw materials than we used. At the beginning of the twentieth century, we produced approximately 15 percent more raw materials for manufactured products than used, but by the middle of the century, we were importing 10 percent more raw materials than we produced.[126] By 1952, we had a critical list of thirty-three minerals, and as has been cited at the beginning of this chapter, many minerals vital to industrial production are imported at a rate higher than the 50 percent level.

It should be apparent that even as we have depleted some of our own minerals, at the present rate of consumption, world resources are not far behind. With 6 percent of the world's population, we use one half of all the world's steel production, more than one half of the world's oil, and about 90 percent of its natural gas. In the twenty years previous to 1961, United States mineral consumption doubled, and it continues to rise. As we come to depend increasingly on mineral imports, we have in truth become a "have not" nation, and only our tremendous industrial wealth, which will rely more and more on outside input, has enabled us to remain prosperous. Dependence on others for basic raw materials can only result in industrial demise. According to Hugo Fisher, administrator of the Resources Agency of California, within fifteen years, with 9½ percent of the world's population, we will be consuming 83 percent of all world raw materials.[127]

One can only wonder what the undeveloped nations of the world will do when they really realize that having depleted our own resources, we are stripping them of their vital resources and potential wealth. Many of the resources, actually almost all, here referred to are non-renewable resources—once used, they are gone. Necessity will eventually force the recycling of many vital minerals, and it is not difficult to think of recycling the metal from junked automobiles and appliances, some of which is recycled already. It is, however, difficult to think of reclaiming mercury from broken thermometers or silver from photographic film. The earth has been pretty well searched and re-searched for mineral wealth and it seems unlikely that any vast new sources will suddenly appear. As we are forced to move to lower-grade ores, procedures for manufacture will become more difficult and expensive.

All the problems discussed in this chapter—the depletion of raw materials, the attendant pollution problems when these raw materials are turned into finished products, and the eventual problem of disposing of the resulting waste—are the result of regarding MAN as the pinnacle of creation, with scarcely a thought being given to the destruction of the fragile ecosystem on which man depends for life and breath. Even now, with spreading alarm over such dilemmas as air and water pollution, it is danger to *man* that is the prime concern—it is merely *unfortunate* that plants and animals are also affected. What is a tree or a bird compared with a *man?* Concern for *man,* rapidly becoming an endangered species (joining the other one thousand as reported in *The Red Book* [the "doomsday book"] by the International World Wildlife Fund), is front and center stage. *Man,* whose ego projected that he had been created in the image of God, *must* be saved.

What is needed now is more than concern for man. What is needed is a compassionate concern for the entire planet and its frail atmosphere, with the full knowledge that unless the entire creation is saved, man, important or not, cannot survive. Attacking the problem piecemeal— air, water, and soil pollution, diminishing open space, etc. —will not get the job done. An effective attack on the entire problem will never occur without a foundational change in value systems. Attacking symptoms will not in the long run save the world. Without a change in our value system, the insects resistant to residual pesticides are likely to inherit the earth.

Altering our value system is going to require the most drastic revision of our life-styles, and a major overhaul of priorities. Ignoring defense spending (not an easy task), one out of three dollars in the past decade going into nondefense capital spending went into highways, which are jammed with 95 million automobiles. That amounts to something like $125 billion for highways, much more than was spent on schools, hospitals, sewer systems. Almost nothing was spent on alleviating automobile emissions. Millions are being spent on the SST, which, as Arthur Godfrey says, we need about as much as we need another load of moon rocks. We spend millions to reimburse oil drillers for their own greedy mistakes to help them clean up oil spills, while our urban and rural poor suffer the most miserable conditions and our environment rapidly deteriorates. It appears that nothing short of an overwhelming disaster will make man understand that far from "having dominion" over the earth, he has fallen fatal victim to his own thoughtless material greed. Where is the necessary dynamic, prophetic leadership to come from to make man realize that careful, thoughtful stewardship of the environment is all that will save the earth and its life? Without that leadership, the prophecy of Martin Litton, director of the Sierra Club, is likely to come true:

> We are prospecting for the very last of our resources and using up the non-renewable things many times faster than we are finding new ones. We've already run out of earth, and nothing we can do will keep humankind in existence for as long as another two centuries.[128]

6

PAST ARBITRATION

Man differs from the "lower" creatures mainly in that he is not locked within the confines of an endowed nature with a fairly fixed repertoire of responses. He possesses, or is possessed by, the freedom to define and shape his own humanity according to the flights of his imagination. He may rise to the heights of love and selflessness, or be the most ruthless of the creatures in cunning self-seeking, and cap it with wanton destruction out of vindictiveness, or even for the sheer hell of it. Man makes himself according to the shape of his notions about the world and his dreams and, as the previous chapters have shown, his dreams may be the most horrible nightmares when they are fully actualized with all their effects accounted for. Even those dreams of yesteryear which were constructive or beneficial in their effects then would not necessarily be so today. Man is part of the evolutionary scene, as his culture vividly shows, thus his plans and dreams must be thoroughly tested before they are deployed, whether they be new and novel or borne along by the weight of tradition. The environmental crises which have been described certainly make vivid the nightmarish qualities of the major dreams (values) of recent Western civilization and the absolute necessity of adopting a new set of values which is ecologically viable.

Consider one vision of technological man for the future: In a recent article, Arthur C. Clarke, the prominent scientist and author of *2001: A Space Odyssey* says he thinks the agricultural age will relatively soon come to an end.[129] Man, he thinks, will soon, in his space technology, develop the potential "to establish self-contained communities *quite independent of agriculture,* anywhere on this planet" that he wishes. Whether or not this is *really* possible seems dubious, but assuming that it is, the real question, as John B. Cobb, Jr., pointed out in a recent lecture,[130] is whether or not man cares enough for the plant and animal world to heal it and adjust himself to its needs, or whether, with his new capability envisioned by Clarke, he might not simply give it up and build for himself vast cities under plastic domes surrounded by poisoned air, polluted water, and sterile rock and dust. The answer to the question is likely largely to be determined by whether or not man goes on worshiping the god that has failed, viz., technology.

The major mischief in man's present world view is his assumption that everything in the world except himself is merely a means to an end and the end is the greater happiness (material welfare) of man. The intellectual pilgrimage of man since the Middle Ages (though certainly with earlier historic roots) has been from the position of seeing his life's goal in the religious image of salvation to a goal of earthly happiness conceived as material welfare and provided by technology. Our future does not lie in a return to the views of the medieval period, even if that were possible. If man is to have a future, it will come through desacralizing technology, recognizing that as a god it has failed, and adopting a set of ways of thinking about God, man, and nature which are ecologically viable; in short, it means a new set of values. These will not by any means be unrelated to the past. We dare not carelessly throw away the heritage of the human race, for as Santayana reminded us, those who do not learn the lessons of history are doomed to repeat them.

The alternatives suggested by Clarke's vision for the future must be faced immediately, for we have, at best estimates, only about one decade in which to reverse our present technological destruction of the biosphere. Will we give it up and vest all our energy in the vain hope that man can create a separate life-support system, or will we devote our energies to healing the biosphere and living within its limited possibilities? The answer to these alternatives is likely to be chosen because of the way man views himself as *in* or *versus* the realm of nature. Is nature an *it* to be used, or is nature in some sense alive and sentient as is man himself? Religiously speaking, is nature also something that God cherishes?

Most of the world's religions have found the principal basis for their belief in a sense of mystery, awe, and wonder derived from the whole fabric of the universe and leading to a sense of assurance about life, a profound inner peace. The Old Testament writers and Christian thinkers after them (and Jewish and Muslim thinkers likewise) have been of a divided mind about the basis for their faith. Some have strongly affirmed that something about history drove them to faith, some personal event or events in the life of a particular people. These thinkers usually pointed to the life of the people Israel, the event Jesus of Nazareth, or Muhammad. History was, in that fashion, narrowly defined as human history. Unconsciously probably at first, the remainder of the world was excluded from God's concern.

Other thinkers of a different school were convinced that all of reality was dominated alike by a Presence which called man to a style of response characterized by humility and universal love. Although the former style of thinkers have dominated Christian thought, this tension never has been fully resolved. From Augustine and Aquinas to Bultmann and Barth, there has been a continuing school of thinkers who call us to consider exclusively human history as the locus from which faith arises. But likewise, from the early mystics through Francis of Assisi to Albert Schweitzer, James Pike, and such crypto-Christians as William James and Alfred North Whitehead, the broader school has remained active with its claim for a Presence dominating all of reality. It is certainly the broader school that can now guide us in developing a theology of ecology. The narrower school, in addition to many other problems of a more technical nature which have led to the "death of God" movement, has been easy game for the implied and specific positivism of the whole scientific movement.

Nonetheless, it was not theology, even bad theology, that killed nature by reducing that living and awesome realm to an "it"; it was, rather, the world view produced by modern science, beginning in the seventeenth century. To appreciate the importance of what was cast aside, we must refer to the writings of some who had not partaken of the particular scientific leaven described above and in the earlier chapters. Theodore Roszak, in *The Making of a Counter Culture*, tells of the reactions of a Wintu Indian woman to what we have done to the environment:

The white people never cared for land or deer or bear. When we Indians kill meat, we eat it all up.

> When we dig roots, we make little hole. . . . We shake down acorns and pinenuts. We don't chop down the trees. We only use dead wood. But the white people plow up the ground, pull up the trees, kill everything. The tree says, "Don't. I am sore. Don't hurt me." But they chop it down and cut it up. The spirit of the land hates them. . . . The Indians never hurt anything, but the white people destroy all. They blast rocks and scatter them on the ground. The rock says, "Don't! You are hurting me." But the white people pay no attention. When the Indians use rocks, they take little round ones for their cooking. . . . How can the spirit of the earth like the white man? . . . Everywhere the white man has touched it, it is sore.[131]

It would never, of course, occur to us to think of trees, rocks, or land as being "sore," or to think at all of any "spirit" of the earth. For us, nature is dead and those creatures which live or vegetate are also merely sentient *things* to be used or abused as man sees fit. The S.P.C.A. has had some effect in reducing the cruelty of man to animals, but the animals certainly are not assumed to have any intrinsic rights compared to man. What is being advocated here is not a return to some form of primitive animism in which "spirits" to be appeased are found in every tree, rock, and spring. But let us consider what more it is that was lost in the construction of modern science after the mechanistic pattern.

The commonsense view of the universe which coalesced by about the seventeenth century took as its primary concept the idea that nature is composed of bits of matter moving about in space which is otherwise empty. Each bit of matter is thought of as a passive fact, an individual reality that does not change through the passage of time. Such matter supports various qualities such as shape, motion, color, odor, all the primary and secondary qualities. Most of what happens in nature is a change in the quality of motion, although there are changes in the other qualities too, but the connection between bits of matter is one of spatial relationships and changes therein. From this, modern notions of geometry arose. Space is eternal and unchanging; all that changes is the relation of bits of matter within space. Added to this picture are the concepts of life and mind which must be accommodated somehow with the other notions. These general observations are taken from Alfred North Whitehead,[132] and he follows it with this:

> The state of modern thought is that every single item in this general doctrine is denied, but that the general conclusions from the doctrine as a whole are tenaciously retained. The result is a complete muddle in scientific thought, in philosophic cosmology, and in epistemology. But any doctrine which does not implicitly presuppose this point of view is assailed as unintelligible.[133]

The principal scientific and philosophical exponents of this point of view are Descartes and Newton. Descartes, working by what he believed was a strict rationalism of deduction from indubitable facts, but who in fact was probably quite dependent upon the commonsense notions, mentioned above, concluded that there are two kinds of substance in the world. The first is thinking substance derived from the recognition of other minds. But the experience of the mind indicates the presence of other unthinking substances, called material bodies; these, Descartes said, are extended substance. He then went on to expound a geometry for space and motion. It was fundamentally Descartes who sundered mind and body, a bifurcation from which we have not yet fully recovered; witness the social scientists who are persistently trying to reduce mind to motion in matter, thereby overcoming Descartes's division.

Most science began to concern itself with Descartes's extended substance, leaving thinking matter to its own devices. A major problem was accounting for the observed effects which bodies separated in space seemed to have upon one another. Here Newton provided not an answer, but a set of laws upon which all further science was based for two centuries, his laws of motion. What was scarcely noticed was that he had not at all given any reason for the law of gravitation. He did not explain the effects observed between bodies, and there is no reason in his concepts of mass and motion why bodies should be so connected. Whitehead observes that Newton "thus illustrated a great philosophic truth, that a dead nature can give no reasons. All ultimate reasons are in terms of aim at value. A dead nature aims at nothing." [134] What we thus obtain, combining Newton with Hume is "a barren concept, namely, a field of perception devoid of any data for its own interpretation, devoid of any reason for the concurrence of its factors." [135]

As Ruth Nanda Anshen has noted,

> Modern science, it is generally admitted, is both the seed and the fruit of the radical spiritual and intellectual revolution which had its birth in the seventeenth century. The child of this revolution in our time is robed in the secularization of consciousness, the denial of transcendent goals, and the sur-

render to immanent aims. We are thus confronted
with a scepticism which is our lonely companion
after the loss of a deeper and more fundamental
process, a process which is life itself.[136]

This skepticism is a pervading form of the modern consciousness. It has not only emptied nature of any worth in
and of itself, but it has emptied man's life of any sense of
meaning or ultimate value. It can lead to a radical, cyni-
cal, and destructive nihilism, or it can lead to a *comparatively* admirable stoic humanism by which a few stalwart
souls manage to get through life. Consider the following
from Bertrand Russell:

> Brief and powerless is man's life; on him and all
> his race the slow sure doom falls pitiless and dark.
> Blind to good and evil, reckless of destruction, omnip-
> otent matter rolls on its relentless way. For man,
> condemned today to lose his dearest, tomorrow him-
> self to pass through the gate of darkness, it remains
> only to cherish, ere yet the blow falls, the lofty
> thoughts that ennoble his little day; disdaining the
> coward terrors of the slave of fate, to worship at the
> shrine that his own hands have built; undismayed by
> the empire of chance, to preserve a mind free from
> the wanton tyranny that rules his outward life;
> proudly defiant of the irresistible forces that tolerate
> for a moment his knowledge and his condemnation,
> to sustain alone, a weary but unyielding Atlas, the
> world that his own ideals have fashioned, despite the
> trampling march of unconscious power.[137]

Certainly the thought of Bertrand Russell expressed in this
passage will be of no help in solving the environmental
crisis. More yet, as Whitehead said, and so clearly demonstrated throughout his writings, the findings of modern
science have undercut their own foundations. Nature has

been reduced to a dull and lifeless affair by science, but only because we have mistaken its high abstractions for normative descriptions of reality and have been willing to neglect the plain evidences of our own lives in order to accept the fruits of science. We need desperately to be reminded that "while nature is complex with timeless subtlety, human thought issues from the simple-mindedness of beings whose active life is less than half a century." [138]

As John Cobb has noted,[139] we persist in rejecting as foolish or superstitious or unproved any psychic "psi factor," despite the fact that the quantity of evidence in its favor and the care expended on its research are far more than enough to establish anything comparable among accepted physical theories. The problem is plainly and simply our bias, even prejudice, against factors that do not accord with the commonsense view derived from science that all facts are based on or derived from sensory perception. Unconsciously, of course, this leads back to the view that the universe is composed of bits of matter moving about in empty space.

Cobb cites as evidence a poll of 352 psychologists taken some years ago regarding their evaluation of ESP—142 believed it was merely an "unknown"; 128 believed it was a remote possibility, and only 31 were favorably disposed to accept it as a reality. In effect, they were saying that no matter what the empirical evidence, so long as it was not explained in terms of sensory perception, the work of psychology on ESP was invalid. This rigorous positivism of these psychologists has perhaps mellowed somewhat in the passing years, since some of the overstatements of positivism are being exposed, and even admitted by avowed positivists such as A. J. Ayer.

Evidence of another nature which should, one thinks,

have led to widespread research has been virtually ignored by psychologists and botanists alike. The Indian botanist, Sir Jagadis Bose measured what can only be described as the pain reaction of plants when they were cut or injured chemically. Although this happened a good sixty years ago, there has been no follow-up research by the scientific community. It apparently would have been too much like accepting the idea that trees and plants were "sore," or that there was a "spirit of the earth," as did the Wintu Indian woman. Recently, an American, Cleve Backster, a former interrogation expert with the CIA, of all things, and a man interested in plant life, was struck with an interesting thought: Why not see if plants give off psychogalvanic energy measurable by lie detector equipment? His first thought was to see if he could measure the rate at which water rose in a plant from the root area into a leaf, using the psychogalvanic reflex index (PGR) as a possible means. After several futile attempts along this line, he began to wonder if there could be a similarity between the tracing from the plant and PGR tracing from a human.

> I decided to obtain a match and burn the plant leaf being tested. At the instant of this decision, . . . there was a dramatic change in the PGR tracing pattern in the form of an abrupt and prolonged upward sweep of the recording pen. I had not moved, or touched the plant, so the timing of the PGR pen activity suggested to me that the tracing might have been triggered by the mere thought of the harm I intended to inflict upon the plant.[140]

Backster further discovered that his plants responded to injury to other life, indicating some undefined perception in the plant. He brought live brine shrimp into the room containing the plants and killed them by dumping them into boiling water. The polygraph needle leaped frantically; clear evidence, apparently, that cells can broadcast their responses to other cells not directly connected in the same organism. Since that date, Backster has conducted many, many more experiments of considerable sophistication, and the results continue to indicate a capability for perception in all living cells and the ability to receive this perception from other cells. He has tested fresh fruits and vegetables, mold cultures, yeasts, scrapings from the roof of the mouth of a person, blood samples, and spermatozoa with the same results.

Most of us, perhaps especially those in the scientific community, will immediately reject this research evidence, refusing to take it seriously. We do so because we have long ago learned "scientifically" that cells don't feel, much less communicate. Nature is dead. Of course, the insensibility of cells has never been proved to us—no one would think to doubt it enough to experiment or demonstrate. Our rejection is thus not really based on any empirical evidence at all, and instead, the commonsense view reigns. We do not reject this new data because it is unintelligible. We have long since accepted the conclusions of physicists regarding subatomic particles and new rays in the electromagnetic spectrum, which we cannot begin to understand. We are, in fact, supposed empiricists, who for dogmatic reasons, reject whatever data does not conform to our dogmas; again, nature is dead—just bits of matter or patterns of energy.

It must be said, of course, that Backster's work may be shown to be in error. In any case, we do well not to be too hasty in reaching conclusions on the basis of an article published in a popular journal, even though the editors, after receiving the article, and because of their own doubts about such matters, visited Backster in his offices and witnessed several experiments. They came away convinced, first, that he is not "some kind of a nut," [141] but a well-qualified man working with care and integrity, and second, that plants do indeed react. Nonetheless, we can rest assured that the general public and the scientific community will expect Backster's experiments to be discredited, and hence, will take no further thought of them; nature is presumed safely dead.

The general name given to the cultural movement that has been dominated by the view of a scientifically dead nature is secularism; philosophically it is called positivism. There is not enough space in this book to analyze either in more detail, but rather we turn to note that a major distinction of world religions has always been their openness to and recognition of a dimension of reality beyond the strictly human and scientific spheres, i.e., they have rejected secularism. Traditional cultic practices and teaching are dramatic or poetic ways of expressing the human awareness of this dimension. They are designed to create in one a sense of wonder at the wholeness of the universe and an awareness of a greater Presence within the process. Under the ruling aegis of the scientific materialistic world view, man's sensitivity to wonder has been reduced to the vanishing point, and any sense of awe at intimations greater than those disclosed through science is treated as superstition.

Can modern man, without sacrificing his honesty or integrity, develop a sense of wonder before the Life in the universe and awe at its Wisdom? There are more than hints that he can. Many great scientists, for example, have transcended the materialistic scientific world view. Whitehead, who has been liberally quoted already, has offered a philosophical scheme for an understanding of the universe in which nature and God are alive and in which wonder is possible. Loren Eiseley, the distinguished anthropologist, like thousands of other scientists, has struggled and found beyond his science a far greater and more wondrous world which makes the best knowledge of his science feeble indeed. Like the poets and saints, these men have learned somehow to open themselves to let the Life of the world speak to them, to hear, beyond their own knowledge, the vast Wisdom of the universe calling them and us to our proper role in the creative advance of the universe. It is a calling to peace and responsibility, to share in the profound joys and sorrows of all life, to appreciate, to create, to heal.

What is clearly needed from theology at this point is a far more adequate doctrine of God than it has traditionally given. It is beyond the scope of this book even to hint at how such a concept of God might be developed, but certainly the philosophy of Alfred North Whitehead can be and is being used as a foundation for a Christian theology in which God is viewed as present in all things, although not in a pantheistic way. Three Americans who have found Whitehead's work of major stimulation are Daniel Day Williams, Schubert M. Ogden, and John B. Cobb, Jr. What is more important for the closure of this book is to understand something of the nature of the man who responds appropriately to the world and the environmental crisis.

His response, whether or not it is evaluated as such, will be religious in nature, albeit not religious in an institutional sense. It is religious in that far more primary sense of awe and wonder before the intimations of the Life

found in the morning dew on a blade of grass shining in
the sun, at the care bestowed by animals upon their young,
at the marvelous balance found in the natural world, and
an amazing suggestion that somehow all that beauty and
care is a display of the real meaning of life. This experience brings an answer to the questions so poignantly
raised by Pascal,

> When I consider the briefness of my life, swallowed
> up in the eternity before and behind it, the small
> space I fill, or even see, engulfed in the infinite im-
> mensity of spaces which I know not, and which know
> not me, I am afraid. . . . Who has set me here? By
> whose order and arrangement have this place and
> this time been allotted me? [142]

It was long ago observed that the perception of the
ultimate cannot be localized either within man or in some
aspect of his environment; it comes to those who look
with open eyes and hearts.

> It is useless to ask whence it comes; there is no
> question of place here. It neither approaches us nor
> withdraws itself; it either manifests itself or remains
> hidden. We must not then seek it, but wait quietly
> for its appearance, and prepare ourselves to contem-
> plate it, as the eye watches for the sun rising above
> the horizon, or out of the sea. . . . The One is every-
> where and nowhere. [143]

This experience is a haunting one which our scientifically blinded minds have been trained to disregard, or
worse yet, to label as superstition or even hallucination.
But the witness of all the ages, and even more importantly
our own experience, is that we cannot state systematically
the logic for our sense of assurance about the meaning of

life, or reduce our experience to precise descriptive statements for replicative experimentation. It is not subject to anything approximating the usual scientific procedures because it transcends all the scientific categories. The appropriate language for relating these experiences is the language of religion, of art, poetry, and drama. But what is captured in these ways can never replace the primary experience itself; it can only reassure one about a present situation, in the light of his own past assurance, concerning life in this universe. As Schubert Ogden has noted, religious assertions do not originate our faith in life's meaning, "but rather provide us with particular symbolic forms through which that faith may be more or less adequately reaffirmed at the level of self-conscious belief." [144]

What religion can do that it has not done, or at best has done very poorly in Western civilization the last two centuries, is to sensitize us to those aspects of life which cannot be encompassed by the scientific world view. For the most part, the Christian churches have been hung up on words and words about words, or on relatively archaic and hence meaningless liturgical patterns. What they seem to have forgotten is that words and liturgy are merely sounds, visual marks or actions intended to refer us to actual life experiences which open us to the present deeper reality of life. What is going on in the world is not words. As Korzybski has put it, we mistake the map for the actual territory. Or as Alan Watts has said, basing life on words and propositions is as futile and barren as eating the menu instead of the dinner. What the church needs is an ecologically viable theology coupled with cultic practices that assist people in opening themselves to the presence of life and of God in all things. We must learn how to keep open the lines of communication between ourselves and the force of life.

When we begin to sense the aliveness of nature and the unifying presence of God in all things, we will be driven to a new set of values, a new ethic, a new set of goals for our lives. We will discover, as Gary Snyder has suggested, that we "must find a way to . . . incorporate the other people—what the Sioux Indians called the creeping people, and the standing people, and the flying people, and the swimming people—into the councils of government. . . . If we don't do it, they will revolt against us. They will submit non-negotiable demands about our stay on earth. We are beginning to get non-negotiable demands right now from the air, the water, the soil." [145]

At the outset, we have much to learn from the primitives, i.e., people untouched by the dubious sophistication of the scientific world view. Synder tells of the way, still today, most Pueblo Indians hunt. They begin their hunt

> by purifying themselves. They take emetics, a sweat bath. . . . They go out hunting in an attitude of humility. They make sure that they need to hunt, that they are not hunting without necessity. Then they improvise a song while they are in the mountains. They sing aloud or hum to themselves while they are walking along. It is a song to the deer, asking the deer to be willing to die for them.[146]

Furthermore, they do not actively hunt for the deer, but wait quietly for a deer to offer itself to them. When the deer has been shot, the head is cut off and placed facing east. Cornmeal is sprinkled in front of the head, and prayer is offered to the deer asking forgiveness for having killed it, explaining the necessity for food and pleading for a good report on the killer to the other deer spirits because of his treatment of the deer. Snyder's point is that we need to find appropriate ways to act in many aspects of our lives to express our response to the presence of life in all things. What is appropriate at the various points of the life cycle: birth, puberty, maturity, marriage, death? How do we adequately sense and express that reverence for life of which Albert Schweitzer spoke and for which he lived?

Alan Watts, in an article telling of his struggles with the need to have reverence for the life of nature and to reconcile that with the need to eat to live, came up with three answers.[147] First, one must face up resolutely and honestly to the fact that if he goes on living it will require killing, whether the death be of animals or vegetables. Given this, the least one can do to appreciate the giving of life for his benefit is to see that the killing is swift, merciful, and reverent. Secondly, every form of life that is to be killed for food must be appropriately cherished. It is, after all, to be incorporated into our bodies, literally to become part of us. The commercialization of food production, whether through hunting or ranching, feed lot or poultry farm, results in flooding the market with unloved creatures. As Watts notes, the typical poultry farm products are nonchickens and pseudoeggs, which were not loved on the farm and hence cannot be loved on the plate. The same lack of reverence results in a fishing industry that is in danger of abolishing fishes and whales by its wholesale slaughter with modern scientific technology. Thirdly, the least that one can do for what has died in his behalf is to cook it to perfection and relish it to the full. Adequate love for plants and animals used for food must include their treatment in the kitchen and in the dining room. Only in ways like these can we express and live in accord with that mysterious assurance that all life, all process, is sacred.

Under the guidance of Darwin and company, however, we have learned to look upon nature and visualize a silent and insatiable war, called the struggle for existence and the survival of the fittest. It was Darwin's view that all of life exhibits basically a selfish struggle in which nothing is modified to serve another species unless it more benefits the first. Charles S. Peirce, in an article called "Evolutionary Love," [148] argues instead that loving cooperation is the basis of evolutionary progress. Nor can anything less, said Peirce, account for the tender emotions experienced by man and the care and sacrifice exhibited in the natural world. Loren Eiseley tells how he finally learned this lesson for himself once and for all. It happened on the beaches of Costabel, where he met and remet the one whom he calls "the star thrower." [149] These beaches typically swarm with shell hunters who, vulture-like, gather not only abandoned shells but occupied living ones by the bagful, which they proceed to plunge into boiling pots, thoughtfully provided by resort hotel operators, to clean specimens. These murdering scavengers are particularly prevalent after storms and early in the day after high tide, hoping to outgrab the other greedy collectors.

Eiseley, avoiding the collectors, proceeded far up the beach one morning after a night storm. Through the early gloom and squally rain he began to make out timbers, conch shells, crabs, sponges, starfish, and various sea creatures cast up on the sand by the storm in considerable number. As the sun began to appear above the horizon behind him, a gigantic rainbow, incredibly perfect, sprang glowing before his view. At its foot, as if in the rainbow, was a human figure who was observed to kneel repeatedly, gaze fixedly at the sand for a time and then rise again. Closing up, Eiseley discovered that this man was seeking out living starfish trapped in the sand or silt and casting them back into their proper realm, the sea. Eiseley, a bit nonplussed by the action, asked the man if he was a collector. His answer: "Only like this. And only for the living. The stars throw well. One can help them." [150]

Slowly, the lesson began to burn itself into Eiseley until at last it took on form; he discovered that he really believed that mercy and love ruled the world, not mere selfish struggle for survival, and his belief began because he himself was possessed by a quite unscientific love of the world and its creatures and by mercy for all the little lost ones. "Red in tooth and claw" nature is not the final word, and man must choose between the way of self-struggle and the way of love. Once more Eiseley sought the star thrower.

> On a point of land, as though projecting into a domain beyond us, I found the star thrower. In the sweet rain-swept morning, that great many-hued rainbow still lurked and wavered tentatively beyond him. Silent I sought and picked up a still-living star, spinning it far out into the waves. I spoke once briefly. "I understand," I said. "Call me another thrower." Only then I allowed myself to think, He is not alone any longer. After us there will be others. [151]

Eiseley proceeded down the beach, experiencing an increasing sense of joy as he cast stars back to live in the sea. Freed at last from Darwin's unceasing struggle, selfishness, and death, he began to experience the love of life and its response to that love. "Somewhere, I felt, in a great atavistic surge of feeling, somewhere the Thrower knew. Perhaps he smiled and cast once more into the boundless pit of darkness. Perhaps he, too, was lonely, and the end toward which he labored remained hidden— even as with ourselves." [152]

Mature religion, i.e., religion that has reached a full and proper, although not final development, since it is dynamic and endless, begins in a profound experience of wonder and awe before the life that is found in every portion of the world and at the majestic Author, present within everything. Religon that fails to appreciate, revere, and care for the manifold life of the world is as deficient as is religion that has no place for an Author and End of all things. The world is aglow with life in all things; that life responds to love; nature is alive! But also, God is present within each element to appreciate and unify the process.

God is not only the Great Lover of the universe, but truly participates in and shares its life feelings, its joys and triumphs, its pain and defeat. God loves the world into each new moment of being, offering to everything its full range of possibilities, totally patient of its own integrity of being, but luring it on by his own aim to its greatest fulfillment. Or better, as Whitehead has said, God "is the poet of the world, with tender patience leading it by his vision of truth, beauty, and goodness." [153] As each moment passes into the next, God weaves its reality and feelings into

the harmony of the universal feeling, which is always immediate, always many, always one, always with novel advance, moving onward and never perishing. The revolts of destructive evil, purely self-regarding, are dismissed into their triviality of merely individual facts; and yet the good they did achieve in individual joy, in individual sorrow, in the introduction of needed contrast, is yet saved by its relations to the completed whole. The image—and it is but an image—the image under which this operative growth of God's nature is best conceived, is that of a tender loving care that nothing be lost.[154]

For the pragmatic realist, dead set on progress through technology, such a view of the world will appear both romantic and fantastic, but as we have tried to show, it alone will allow the continuance of life for mankind. The pragmatic realist, with his god of technology and his goal of material welfare, is murdering the earth. We need a radically new vision of man, and a social order that rewards the man who loves and cares for the world—man who refuses to grasp after power in order to use it to manipulate the world or persons for his own personal benefit. As was observed, especially in connection with the Frontier, in our history we have mostly followed the vision of the man who gets power and uses it to benefit himself, who ravishes nature to reap its riches. We *honor* those occasional heroes of history who have rejected this pattern and instead have used their power only to free others for a more fully human existence—men like Jesus, Buddha, Moses, Muhammad, or Francis of Assisi. Yet, is not our honor for them mostly with words and not with the history-making deeds of our lives? Imitation is not only the sincerest form of flattery, it is the only sincere form of honor.

Measured by this rule, our real praise is reserved for the powerful men of history cut to the pattern of the Alexanders, Caesars, Napoleons, men like John D. Rockefeller, Carnegie, Mellon, Teddy Roosevelt, or Joseph Kennedy. The incredible power of our technology to destroy the biosphere will not permit us another generation of this folly. We must be done once and for all with the views and desires that give high priority to the conquest of others and of nature. The man who *needs* power, for whatever reason, is not the man of the future, but the man whose future is past. There is no room for him in this world. His vision is depraved and he is not really suited for life, much less for leadership in our delicately balanced world. Leave power in the hands of this kind of man and he will make ours the age in which T. S. Eliot's words come true, the age that "advances progressively backwards." He is a man like some of our political and military leaders who believe that by destroying Vietnam, and then Cambodia, we are really saving them. He can act vacuously, without questioning, to sacrifice the natural world to increase man's riches. He cooperates fully with the society whose propensity seems to be the inundation of itself with its own waste products.

Any amelioration of the environmental crisis, much less its reversal, will require the dominance of a new set of purposes for man and a new style for his society, which recognizes and values the life that is everywhere present and which is organized to facilitate an appropriate response by the individual. This can mean nothing less than a religious and cultural renaissance of more sweeping proportions than the cultural renaissance that ended the Middle Ages. It will mean a serious and commanding humility about man and his technological prowess. We can never again afford to neglect the Wisdom which calls to us from the universe, simply in order to deploy our vast and destructive schemes of control. That Wisdom calls us to find meaning in life itself, not in the exploitation of the material resources which surround it. The producer-consumer society in which we exist to make a profit from one another is not only inherently destructive of the physical world; basically it is morally disastrous. It elevates and rewards greed and renders loving care impotent. Human meaning is most fully realized when man knows himself as the guardian and steward of life in the world; his role is to appreciate and care for the beauty of life in all things.

Can we hope for an end to this age in which "things are in the saddle and ride mankind"? It *will* end. Because it is unnatural, it cannot last. We can hope that Charles Peirce was right in his vision of the future given in a lecture in 1863:

> When the conclusion of our age comes, and skepticism and materialism have done their perfect work, we shall have a far greater faith than ever before. For then man will see God's wisdom and mercy, not only in every event of his own life, but in that of the gorilla, the lion, the fish, the polyp, the tree, the crystal, the grain of dust, the atom. He will see that each one of these has an inward existence of its own, for which God loves it, and that He has given to it a nature of endless perfectibility. He will see the folly of saying that nature was created for his use. He will see that God has no other creation than his children.[155]

NOTES

1. Ian L. McHarg, *Design with Nature* (The Natural History Press, 1969), pp. 44 f.

2. Loren Eiseley, *The Immense Journey* (Time, Inc., 1962), p. 36.

3. *Ibid.*

4. *Ibid.*, p. 38.

5. Gerhard von Rad, *Old Testament Theology,* Vol. I, tr. by D. M. G. Stalker (Harper & Row, Publishers, Inc., 1962), p. 146.

6. *Ibid.*, p. 152.

7. C. F. von Weizsäcker, *The History of Nature,* tr. by Fred D. Wieck (The University of Chicago Press, 1949), p. 67.

8. *Ibid.*, pp. 52 f.

9. *Ibid.*, pp. 58 f.

10. R. H. Tawney, *Religion and the Rise of Capitalism* (Harcourt, Brace and Company, 1926; Mentor edition, 1953), pp. 228 f.

11. *Ibid.*, p. 34.

12. *Ibid.*, p. 35.

13. Quoted in *ibid.*, p. 38.

14. "Declining Mortality," *Lancet,* Oct. 26, 1963, p. 870.

15. Roscoe Spencer, "Individual and Species: Biological Survival," *The Subversive Science: Essays Toward an Ecology of Man,* ed. by Paul Shepard and Daniel McKinley (Houghton Mifflin Company, 1969), pp. 93 ff.

16. Lynn White, Jr., "The Historical Roots of Our Ecologic Crisis," *ibid.*, p. 348.

17. Gerhard von Rad, *Old Testament Theology*, Vol. II, tr. by D. M. G. Stalker (Harper & Row, Publishers, Inc., 1965), p. 146.

18. Cf. *ibid., passim.*

19. Von Rad, *op. cit.*, Vol. I, p. 441.

20. *Ibid.*, p. 450.

21. Raymond E. Brown, ed. and tr., *The Gospel According to John* (Doubleday & Company, Inc., The Anchor Bible, Vol. 29, 1966), p. cxxii.

22. Quoted in J. B. Bury, *The Idea of Progress* (Dover Publications, Inc., 1955), p. 173.

23. *Ibid.*, p. 176.

24. Walter Prescott Webb, *The Great Frontier* (Houghton Mifflin Company, 1952), p. 340.

25. Robert Heilbroner, *The Worldly Philosophers* (Time, Inc., 1962), p. 66.

26. Francis Bowen, *American Political Economy* (first published in 1856), quoted in Russell B. Nye, *This Almost Chosen People* (Michigan State University Press, 1966), p. 125.

27. Garrett Hardin, "Interstellar Migration and the Population Problem," *Heredity*, Vol. 50 (1959), pp. 68-70.

28. Kenneth Boulding, *The Meaning of the Twentieth Century* (Harper & Row, Publishers, Inc., 1964), p. 125.

29. *Ibid.*

30. Paul R. Ehrlich, *The Population Bomb* (Ballantine Books, Inc., 1968), p. 38.

31. *Ibid.*, p. 27.

32. William and Paul Paddock, *Famine—1975!* (Little, Brown and Company, 1967), p. 16.

33. *Ibid.*

34. Ehrlich, *op. cit.*, p. 86.

35. William C. Paddock, "How Green Is the Green Revolution?" (mimeographed, prepared for *BioScience*, 1970), pp. 13 f.

36. Wayne H. Davis, "Overpopulated America," *New Republic*, Vol. 162, No. 2, Issue 2872 (Jan. 10, 1970), p. 31.

37. Garrett Hardin, "The Tragedy of the Commons," from *Science*, Vol. 162 (Dec. 13, 1968), p. 1234; reprinted in *The Environmental Handbook*, ed. by Garrett DeBell (Ballantine Books, Inc., 1970), p. 31.

38. *Ibid.*, p. 37.

39. Robert and Leona Train Rienow, *Moment in the Sun* (Ballantine Books, Inc., 1967), p. 275.

40. *Ibid.*, p. 276.

41. *Ibid.*, p. 277.

42. *Ibid.*, Ch. XII, n. 6, p. 346.

43. Ehrlich, *op. cit.*, p. 83.

44. *Ibid.*, p. 145.

45. Alfredo Aguirre, report in *The Population Council*, quoted in David Lyle, "The Human Race Has Maybe Thirty-five Years Left," *Esquire*, Sept., 1967.

46. Philip Appleman, *The Silent Explosion*, quoted in Lyle, *loc. cit.*

47. Louis T. Kardos, "A New Prospect," *Environment*, Vol. 12, No. 2 (March, 1970), p. 10.

48. Barry Commoner, "Duty of Science in the Ecological Crisis," *Scientist and Citizen* (now *Environment*), Vol. 9, No. 8 (Oct., 1967), p. 173.

49. Paddock and Paddock, *op. cit.*, p. 46.

50. Facts concerning the "California Water Plan" were taken from an article by Frank M. Stead, "Desalting California," printed originally in the Spring, 1969, issue of *Cry California*, published by California Tomorrow, and reprinted in *Environment*, Vol. 11, No. 5 (June, 1969), p. 2.

51. Jules B. Billard, "The Revolution in American Agriculture," *National Geographic*, Vol. 137, No. 2 (Feb., 1970), p. 177.

52. *Ibid.*, pp. 160 f.

53. Lyle, *loc. cit.*

54. "Poisoning the Wells," Staff Report, *Environment*, Vol. 11, No. 1 (Jan.-Feb., 1969), p. 16.

55. Harmon Henkin, "Side Effects," *Environment*, Vol. 11, No. 1, pp. 28 ff.

56. "Diminishing Returns," Staff Report, *Environment*, Vol. 11, No. 7 (Sept., 1969), p. 6.

57. Kevin Shea, "Cotton and Chemicals," *Environment*, Vol. 10, No. 9 (Nov., 1968), pp. 209 ff.

58. *Ibid.*

59. Kevin Shea, "Unwanted Harvest," *Environment*, Vol. 11, No. 7 (Sept., 1969), p. 16.

60. "Soviet Use of Pesticides Cited in Wildlife Slaughter," Associated Press news release, *St. Louis Globe-Democrat*, April 27, 1970.

61. Justin Frost, "Earth, Air and Water," *Environment*, Vol. 11, No. 6 (July-Aug., 1969), p. 21.

62. Kenneth E. F. Watt, "Whole Earth," *Earth Day—The Beginning* (Bantam Book, May, 1970), pp. 20 f.

63. Lyle, *loc. cit.*

64. Paddock and Paddock, *op. cit.,* p. 130.

65. W. C. Paddock, *loc. cit.*, p. 7.

66. *Ibid.*

67. *Ibid.*, p. 6.

68. Paul Ehrlich, "The Food-from-the-Sea Myth," *Saturday Review*, April 4, 1970, p. 53.

69. *Ibid.*

70. Rienow and Rienow, *op. cit.*, p. 248.

71. Webb, *op. cit.*, p. 292.

72. Rienow and Rienow, *op. cit.*, p. 37.

73. Charles F. Park, Jr., ed., in collaboration with Margaret C. Freeman, *Affluence in Jeopardy* (Freeman, Cooper & Co., 1968), pp. 12 ff.

74. Dean E. Abrahamson, *Environmental Cost of Electric Power* (Scientists' Institute for Public Information Workbook, 1970), p. 30.

75. *Ibid.*, p. 6.

76. *Ibid.*, p. 7.

77. "The Space Available," A Report from the Committee for Environmental Information, *Environment*, Vol. 12, No. 2 (March, 1970), p. 2.

78. Abrahamson, *op. cit.*, p. 11.

79. Richard Curtis and Elizabeth Hogan, *The Perils of the Peaceful Atom* (Ballantine Books, Inc., 1969), p. 257.

80. *Ibid.*, pp. 257 f.

81. *Ibid.*, p. 115.

82. *Ibid.*, p. 107.

83. *Ibid.*, p. 108.

84. *Ibid.*

85. *Ibid.*, p. 110.

86. *Ibid.*, pp. 193 f.

87. *Ibid.*, p. 305.

88. *Ibid.*, pp. 143 ff.

89. Abrahamson, *op. cit.*, p. 16.

90. *Ibid.*

91. Bertram W. Carnow, "Pollution Invites Disease," *Saturday Review,* July 4, 1970, p. 38.

92. "Ecologists in the Mekong," *New Republic,* Vol. 162, No. 13, Issue 2883 (March 28, 1970), pp. 6 f.

93. Rienow and Rienow, *op. cit.*, p. 73.

94. Ed Chaney, "Too Much for the Columbia River Salmon," *National Wildlife*, Vol. 8, No. 3 (April-May, 1970), p. 19.

95. *Ibid.*

96. Don Wooldridge and Mark Sullivan, "Pollution," *Missouri Conservationist*, Vol. 31, No. 7 (July, 1970), p. 8.

97. Wesley Marx, *The Frail Ocean* (Ballantine Books, Inc., 1967), p. 93.

98. *Ibid.*, p. 88.

99. *Ibid.*, p. 89.

100. *Ibid.*, p. 96.

101. "Demand Is Growing for Low-Sulfur Oil," Associated Press news release, *St. Louis Post-Dispatch,* July 21, 1970, p. 9A.

102. Ralph E. Lapp, "Where Will We Get the Energy?" *New Republic*, Vol. 163, No. 2, Issue 2898 (July 11, 1970), p. 17.

103. Park and Freeman, eds., *op. cit.*, p. 200.

104. Lapp, *loc. cit.*, p. 20.

105. Carol Collier, "On Breathing Sulfur Dioxide," *Scientist and Citizen* (now *Environment*), Vol. 10, No. 9 (Nov., 1968), p. 220.

106. Carnow, *loc. cit.*, p. 39.

107. *Air Pollution,* Committee Report for Scientists' Institute for Public Information, 1970, p. 7.

108. "Fighting to Save the Earth from Man," *Time,* Feb. 2, 1970.

109. Jean Mayer, "Scientific Questions, Toward a Non-Malthusian Population Policy," *Hunger* (Scientists' Institute for Public Information Workbook, 1970), p. 19.

110. Samuel Brody, "Facts, Fables, and Fallacies on Feeding the World Population," in Shepard and McKinley, eds., *op. cit.*, p. 71.

111. Robert and Leona Train Rienow, "The Age of Eternal Twilight," *Audubon*, Vol. 72, No. 4 (July, 1970), p. 4.

112. *Ibid.*

113. *Ibid.*, p. 6.

114. *Ibid.*

115. *Ibid.*

116. William O. Douglas, "Their Glory Is in Danger," *Holiday*, May, 1968.

117. Marx, *op. cit.*, pp. 63 ff.

118. *Ibid.*, p. 65.

119. *Ibid.*, p. 67.

120. Maurice Franz, "Two Kinds of June," *Organic Gardening*, June, 1970, p. 76.

121. Marx, *op. cit.*, p. 72.

122. William Murdoch and Joseph Connell, "All About Ecology," *The Center Magazine*, Vol. III, No. 1 (Jan., 1970), p. 62.

123. George McCue, "Will Our Refuse Bury Us?" *St. Louis Post-Dispatch*, Jan. 18, 1970.

124. "Fighting to Save the Earth from Man," *loc. cit.*

125. Garrett DeBell, "Recycling," in DeBell, ed., *op. cit.*, p. 214.

126. Rienow and Rienow, *op. cit.*, p. 19.

127. *Ibid.*, p. 20.

128. "Fighting to Save the Earth from Man," *loc. cit.*

129. Arthur C. Clarke, "Beyond Babel 2," *Youth*, June 7, 1970.

130. John B. Cobb, Jr., "The Population Explosion and the Rights of the Subhuman World" (mimeographed, April, 1970).

131. Theodore Roszak, *The Making of a Counter Culture* (Doubleday Anchor Book, 1969), p. 245.

132. Alfred North Whitehead, *Modes of Thought* (The Macmillan Company, 1938), pp. 174 f.

133. *Ibid.*, p. 180.

134. *Ibid.*, p. 184.

135. *Ibid.*

136. Ruth Nanda Anshen, ed., *Alfred North Whitehead, His Reflections on Man and Nature* (Harper & Brothers, 1961), p. 1.

137. Bertrand Russell, *Mysticism and Logic* (London: George Allen and Unwin Ltd., 1917), pp. 56 f.

138. Anshen, ed., *op. cit.*, p. 45.

139. Cobb, *op. cit.*, pp. 19 ff.

140. Thorne Bacon, "The Man Who Reads Nature's Signals," *National Wildlife,* Vol. 7, No. 2 (Feb.-March, 1969), pp. 6 f.

141. *Ibid.*, p. 8.

142. Blaise Pascal, *Pensées,* tr. by Rawlings, in *Selected Thoughts* (Scott Library, XCV), p. 48.

143. Plotinus, *The Way of Mysticism,* ed. by Joseph James (Harper & Brothers, 1951), p. 47.

144. Schubert M. Ogden, *The Reality of God and Other Essays* (Harper & Row, Publishers, Inc., 1966), pp. 23 ff.

145. Gary Snyder, "The Wilderness and the Non-Verbal," *The Center Magazine*, Vol. III, No. 4 (July, 1970), p. 70.

146. *Ibid.*, p. 71.

147. Alan Watts, "Murder in the Kitchen," *Playboy,* Dec., 1969, p. 225.

148. Charles S. Peirce, "Evolutionary Love," *Chance, Love and Logic* (Barnes & Noble, Inc., 1968 [original, 1923]), pp. 267 ff.

149. Loren Eiseley, *The Unexpected Universe* (Harcourt, Brace and World, Inc., 1964), pp. 67 ff.

150. *Ibid.*, p. 72.

151. *Ibid.*, p. 89.

152. *Ibid.*, p. 91.

153. Alfred North Whitehead, *Process and Reality* (Humanities Press, Inc., 1929), p. 526.

154. *Ibid.*, p. 525.

155. Charles S. Peirce, "The Place of Our Age in the History of Civilization," *Values in a Universe of Chance* (Doubleday Anchor Book, 1958), p. 13.